Oshawa Ontario Book 3 in Colour Photos, Saving Our History One Photo at a Time

Photography by Barbara Raué
©2018

Series Name: Cruising Ontario

Book 206: Oshawa Book 3

Cover photo: 18 Aberdeen Street, Page 20

©All the photos in this book have been taken with my cameras. I own the rights to them.

Series Name: Cruising Ontario
Saving Our History One Photo at a Time
in colour photos

Books Available in Alphabetical Order:
Aberfoyle, Acton, Ajax, Alton, Amherstburg, Ancaster, Arthur, Auburn, Aylmer, Ayr, Beaver Valley, Belgrave, Belleville, Bloomingdale, Blyth, Brantford, Brockville, Burford, Burlington, Caledon, Caledonia, Cambridge, Carlow, Chatsworth, Clifford, Collingwood, Conestogo, Delhi, Dorchester to Aylmer, Drayton, Drumbo, Dundas, Dunlop, Eden Mills, Elmira, Elora, Erin, Essex, Fergus, Goderich, Grimsby, Guelph, Hagersville, Hamilton, Hanover, Harriston, Hespeler, Jarvis, Kingston, Kingsville, Kitchener, Lake Superior, Lincoln, Linwood, Listowel, London, Lucknow, Merrickville, Mono, Mount Forest, Mount Pleasant, Neustadt, New Hamburg, Newboro, Newport, Niagara-on-the-Lake, Oakville, Onondaga, Orangeville, Orillia, Oshawa, Owen Sound, Palmerston, Paris, Pelham, Perth, Peterborough, Petrolia, Pickering, Port Colborne, Port Elgin, Portland, Preston, Rockwood, Sarnia, Sault Ste. Marie, Seaforth, Sheffield, Shelburne, Simcoe, Smiths Falls, Smithville, Southampton, St. Catharines, St. George, St. Jacobs, St. Marys, St. Thomas, Stoney Creek, Stratford, Thamesford, Thunder Bay, Tillsonburg, Toronto, Waterdown, Waterford, Waterloo, Welland, Wellesley, West Flamborough, Westport, Whitby, Windsor, Wingham, Woodstock

Book 200: West Flamborough
Book 201-202: Whitby
Book 203: Ajax and Pickering
Book 204-206: Oshawa

Table of Contents

Brock Street East — Page 6

Brock Street West — Page 12

McMillan Drive — Page 16

Alma Street — Page 18

Hospital Court — Page 18

Aberdeen Street — Page 20

Connaught Street — Page 25

Mary Street North — Page 36

Grierson Street — Page 43

Rossland Road East — Page 45

Masson Street — Page 48

Oshawa is a city in Southern Ontario on the Lake Ontario shoreline. It is about sixty kilometres east of Downtown Toronto. The name Oshawa comes from the Ojibwa word meaning "the crossing place" or "where we must leave our canoes". More than 5,000 people work and more than 2,400 university students study in the downtown core.

Oshawa's roots are tied to the automobile industry with the Canadian division of General Motors located here. It was founded in 1876 as the McLaughlin Carriage Company. The lavish home of the carriage company's founder, Parkwood Estate, is a National Historic Site of Canada.

Historians believe that Oshawa began as a transfer point for the fur trade. Beaver and other animals trapped for their pelts by local natives were traded with the Coureurs des bois (voyagers). Furs were loaded onto canoes by the Mississauga Indians at the Oshawa harbor and transported to the trading posts located to the west at the mouth of the Credit River. Around 1760, the French constructed a trading post near the harbor location; this was abandoned after a few years, but its ruins provided shelter for the first residents of what later became Oshawa.

In the late eighteenth century a local resident, Roger Conant, started an export business shipping salmon to the United States. His success attracted further migration into the region. A large number of the founding immigrants were United Empire Loyalists, who left the United States to live under British rule. Later Irish and then French Canadian immigration increased as did industrialization. Oshawa and the surrounding Ontario County were the settling grounds of a large number of nineteenth century Cornish immigrants. The surveys ordered by Governor John Graves Simcoe, and subsequent land grants, helped populate the area. When Col. Asa Danforth laid out his York-to-Kingston road, it passed through the Oshawa area.

In 1822, a "colonization road" (a north-south road to facilitate settlement) known as Simcoe Street was constructed. It ran from the harbor to the area of Lake Scugog. It intersected the "Kingston Road: at what became Oshawa's "Four Corners."

In 1846 there were about 1,000 people in a community surrounded by farms. There were three churches, a post office, various types of tradesmen, a foundry, a grist mill and a fulling mill, a brewery, two distilleries, a machine shop and four cabinet makers.

The newly established village became an industrial center, and implement works, tanneries, asheries and wagon factories opened. In 1876, Robert Samuel McLaughlin, Sr. moved his carriage works to Oshawa from Enniskillen to take advantage of its harbor and of the availability of a rail link not too far away. He constructed a two-storey building, which was soon added to. This building was heavily remodeled in 1929, receiving a new facade and being extended to the north. Around 1890, the carriage works relocated from its Simcoe Street address to an unused furniture factory a couple of blocks to the northeast, and this remained its site until the building burnt in 1899. Offered assistance by the town, McLaughlin chose to stay in Oshawa, building a new factory across Mary Street from the old site. Rail service had been provided in 1890 by the Oshawa Railway; this was originally set up as a streetcar line, but by about 1910 a second freight line was built slightly to the east of Simcoe Street which provided streetcar and freight service, connected central Oshawa with the Grand Trunk (now Canadian National) Railway, and with the Canadian Northern (which ran through the very north of Oshawa) and the Canadian Pacific, built in 1912-13.

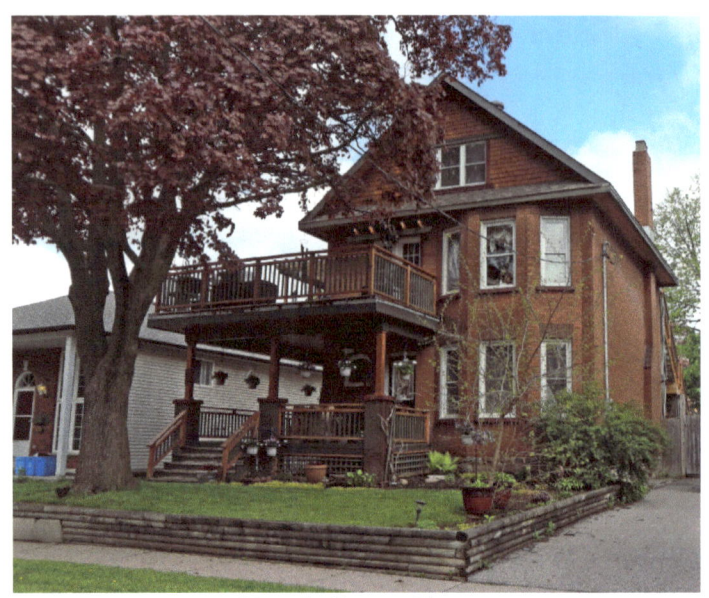

Brock Street East

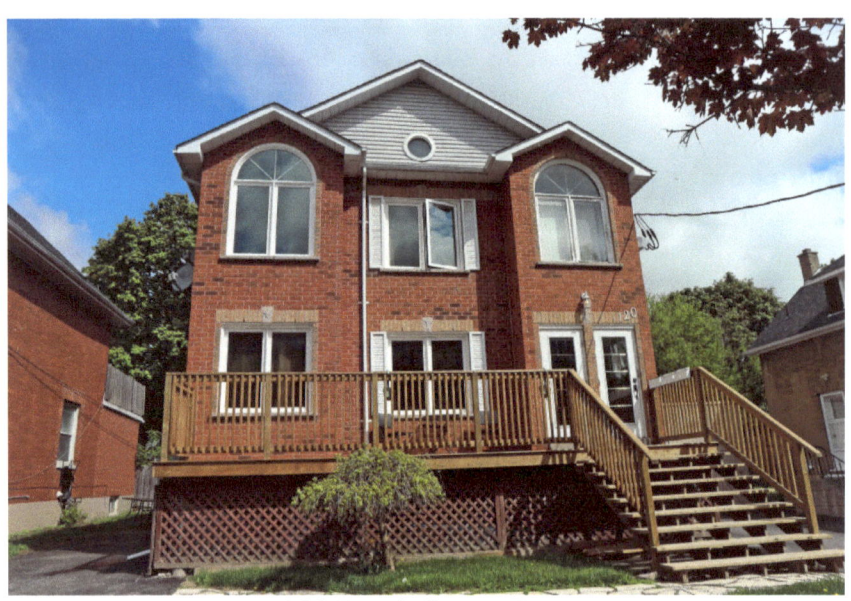

120 Brock Street East

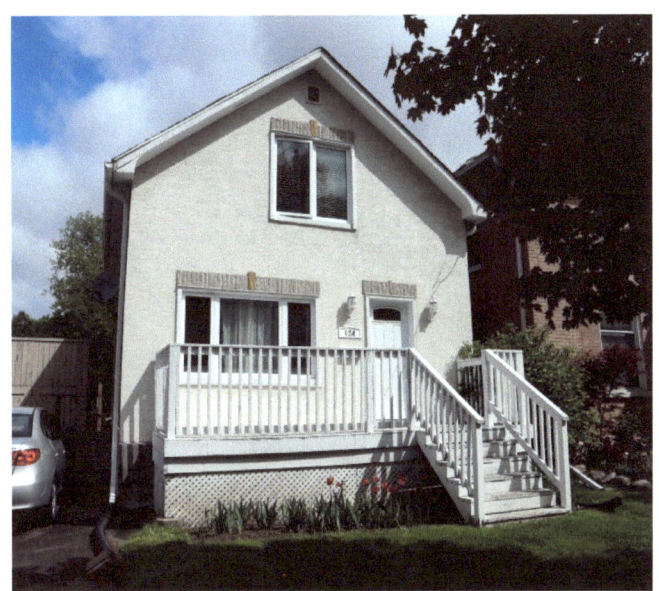

124 Brock Street East

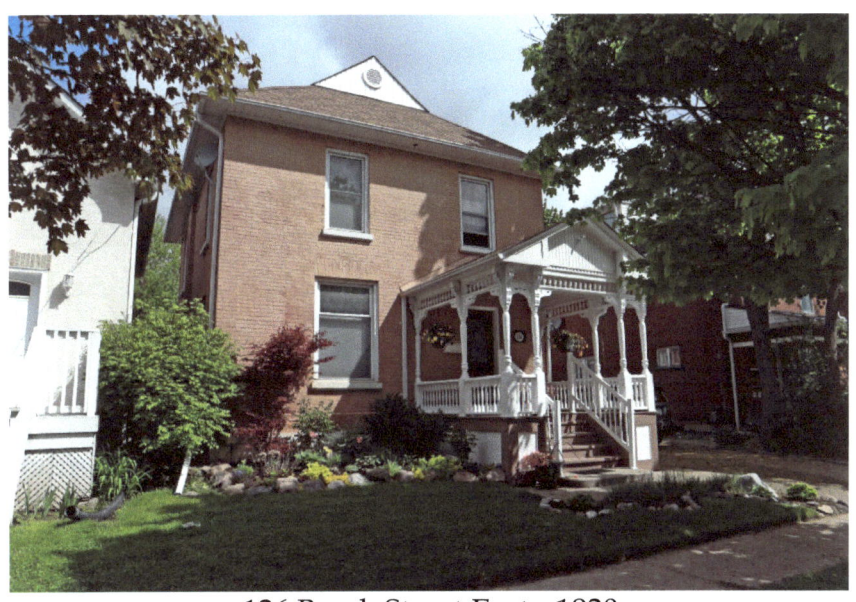

126 Brock Street East - 1920

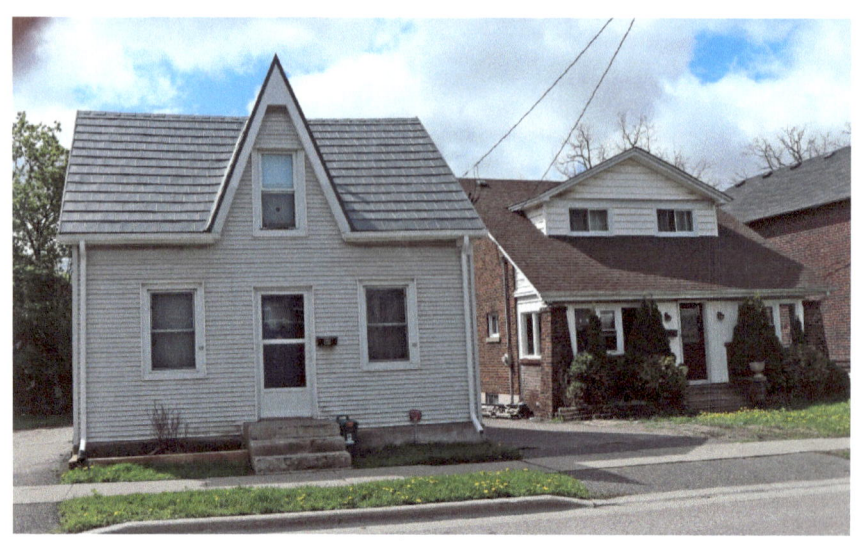

69 Brock Street East

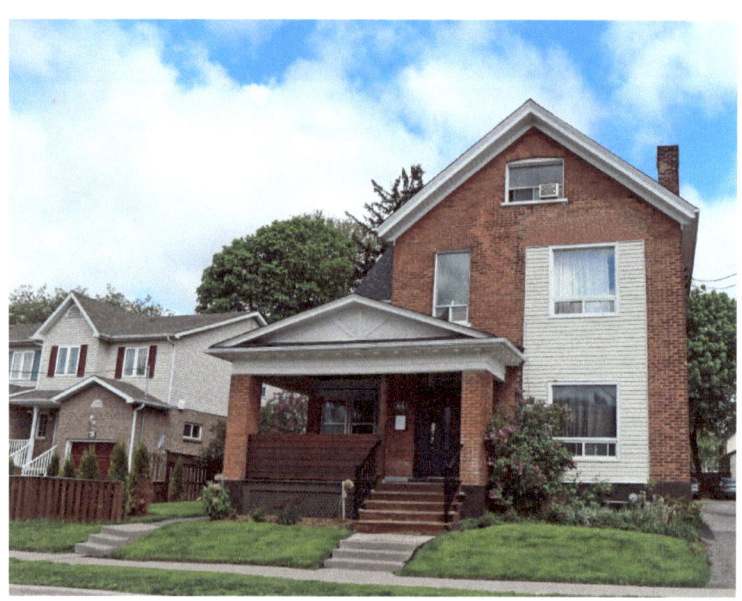

64 Brock Street East - 1910

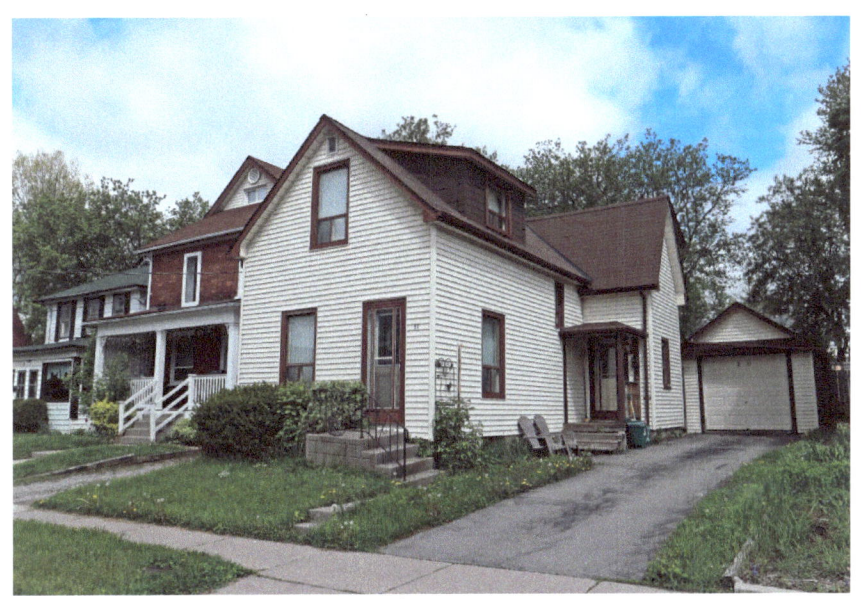

50 Brock Street East

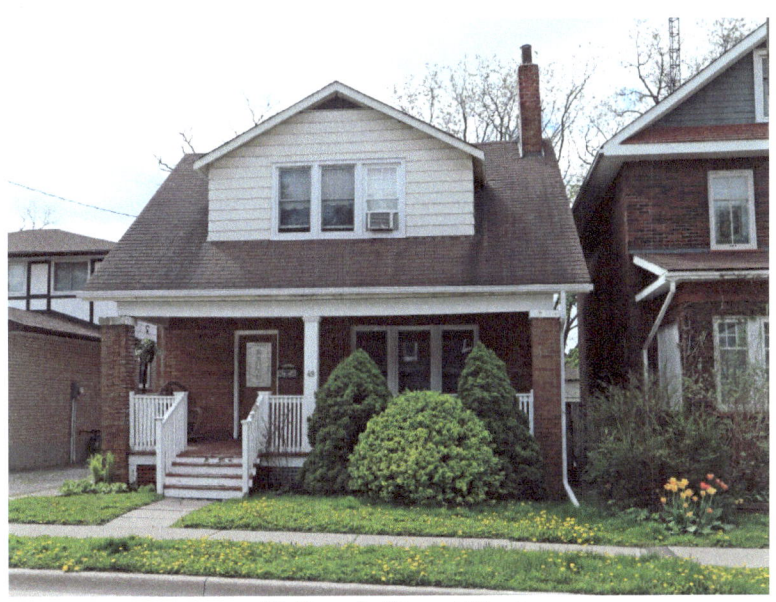

49 Brock Street East

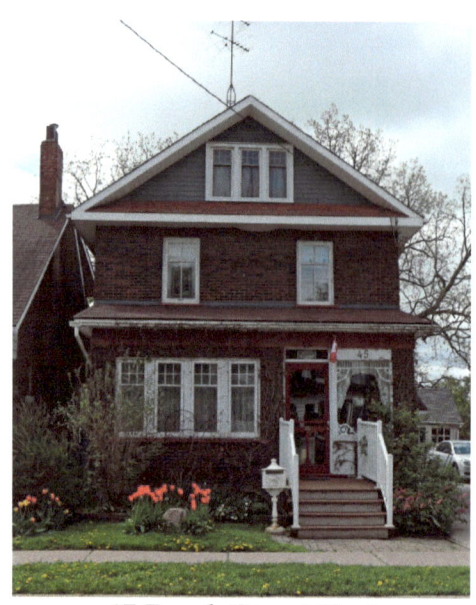

45 Brock Street East

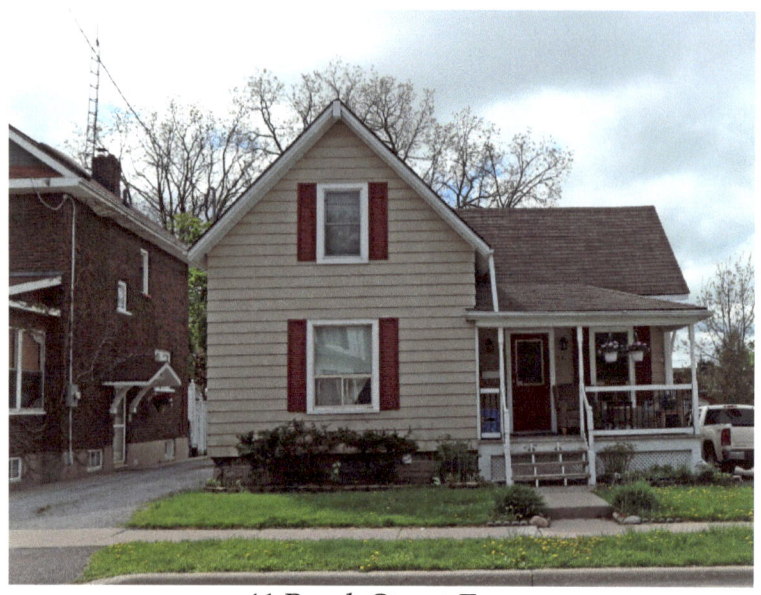

41 Brock Street East

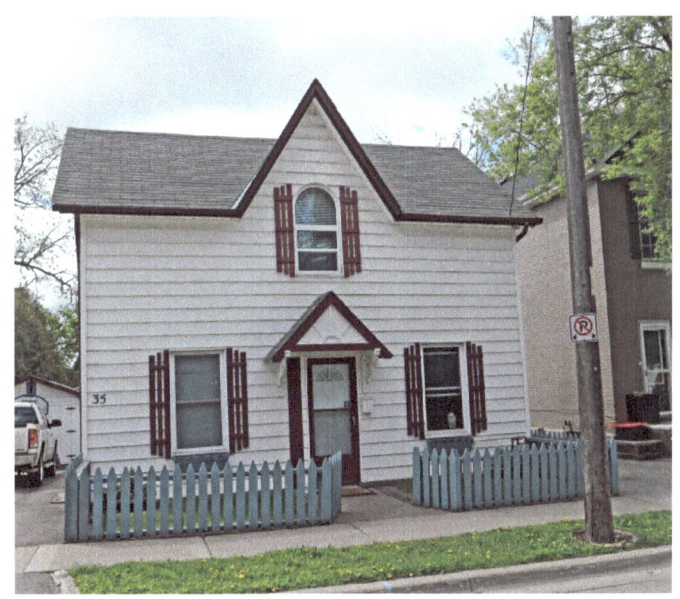

35 Brock Street East - 1900

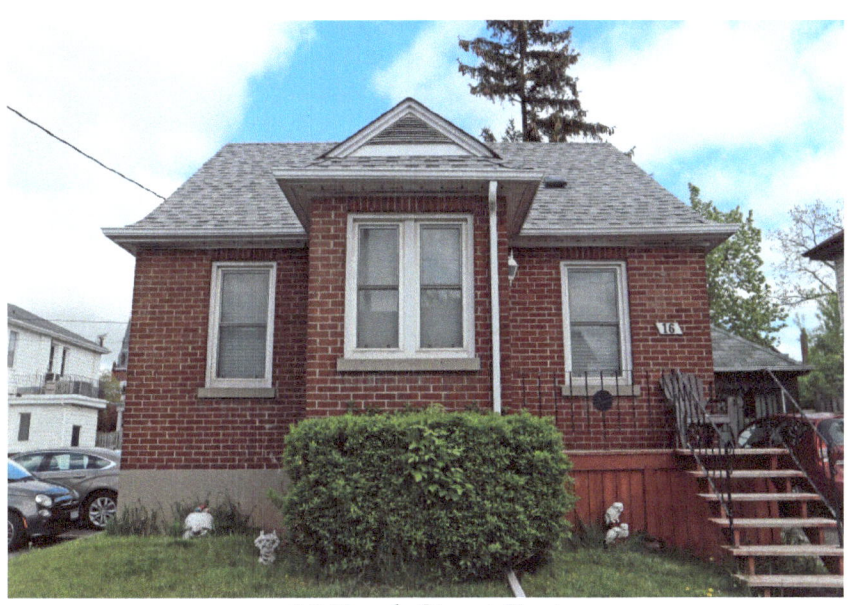

16 Brock Street East

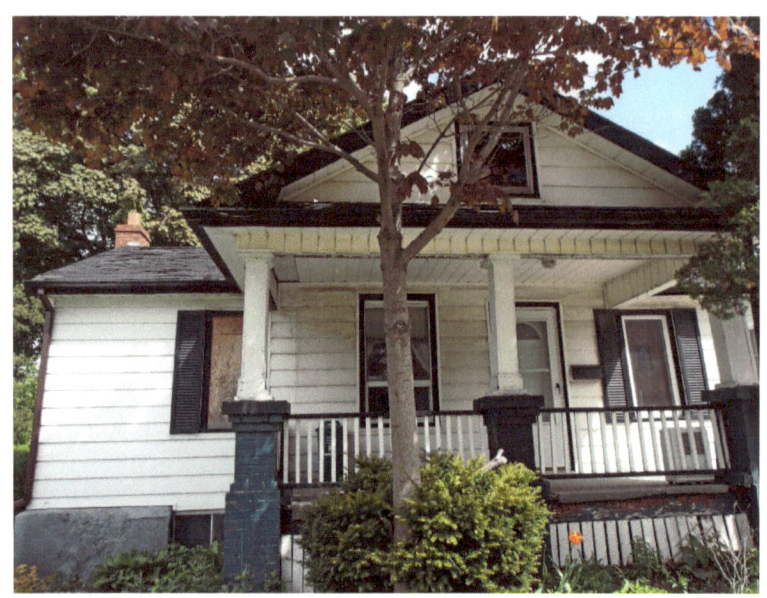

118 Brock Street West - 1860

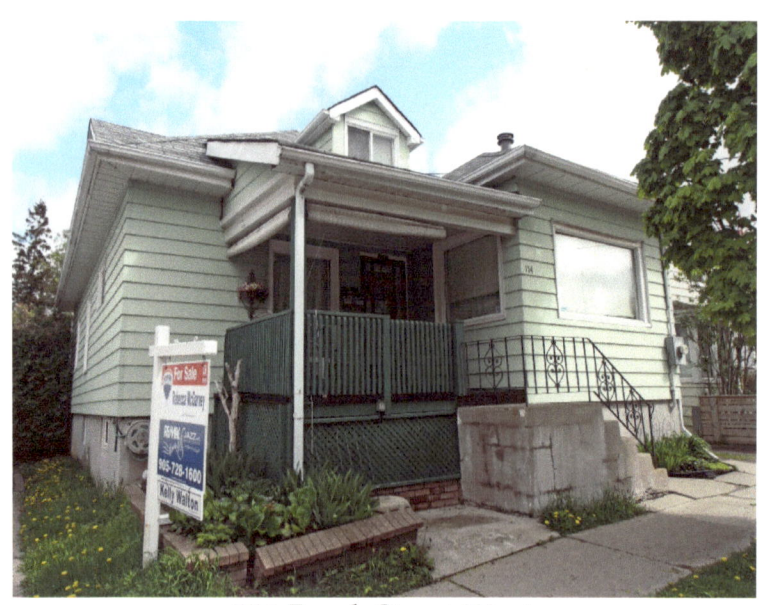

114 Brock Street West

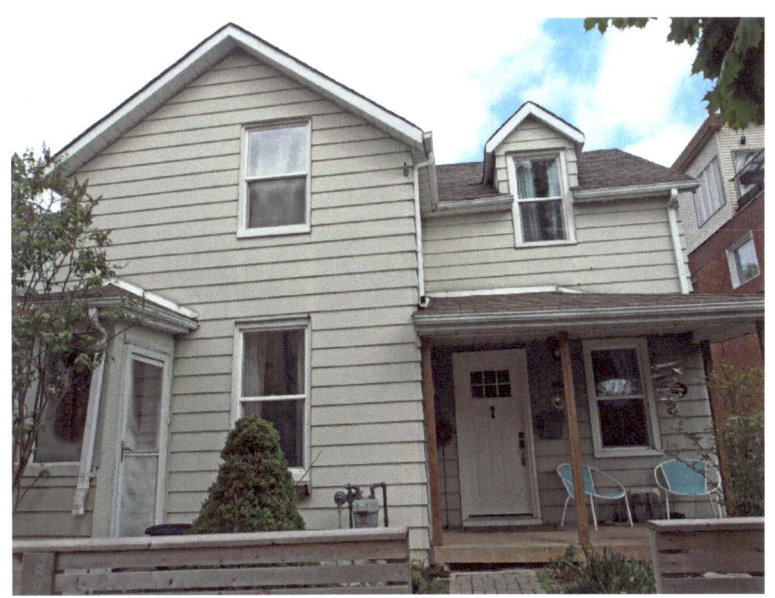

110 Brock Street West

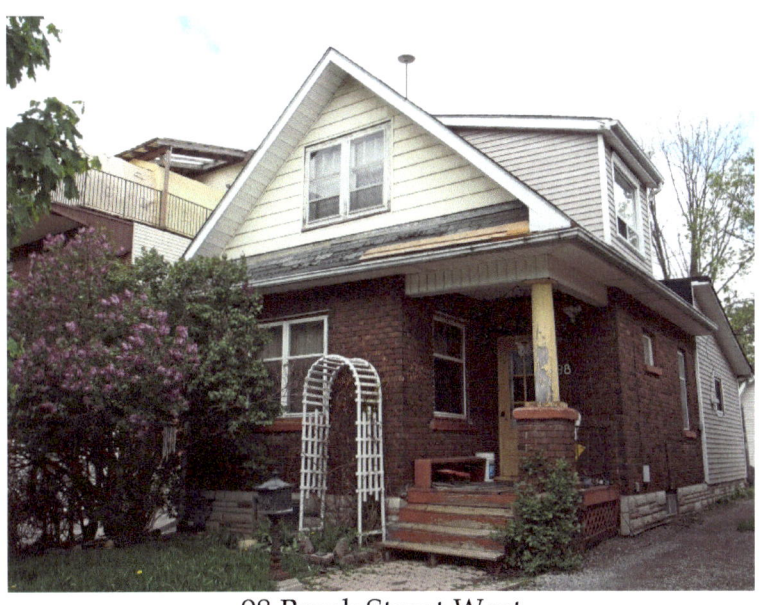

98 Brock Street West

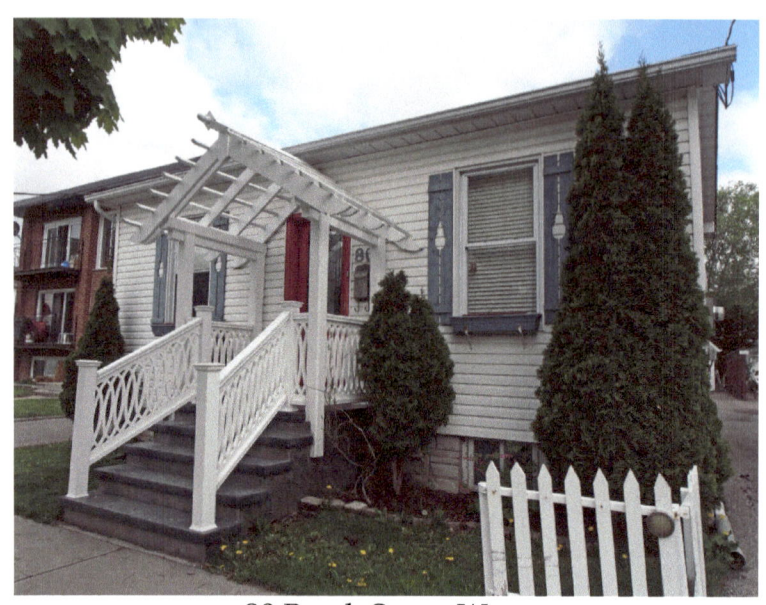

80 Brock Street West

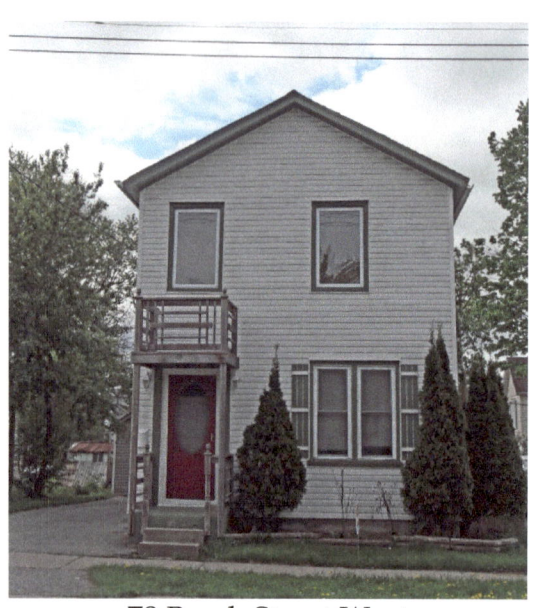

79 Brock Street West

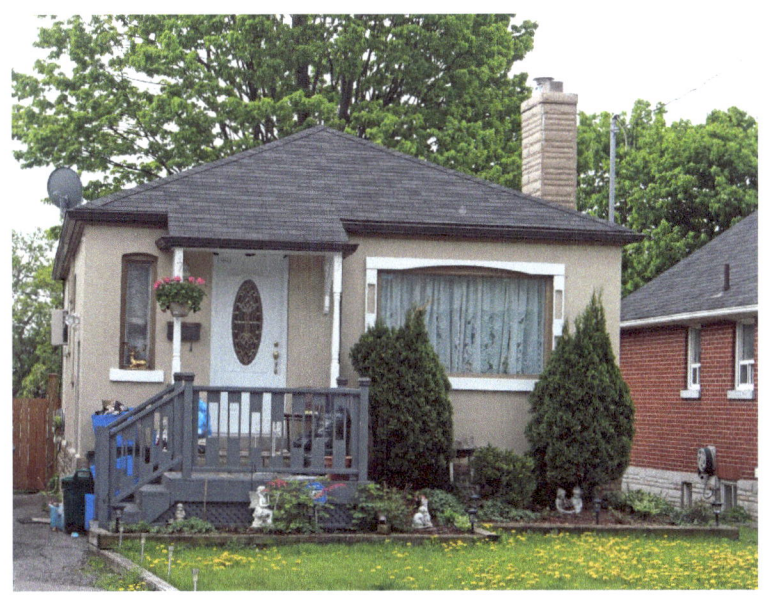

Brock Street West

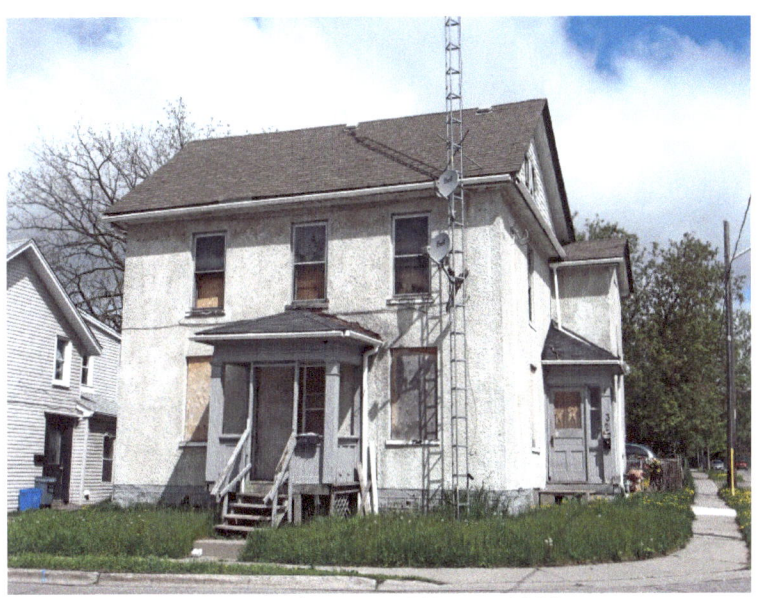

32 Brock Street West - 1890

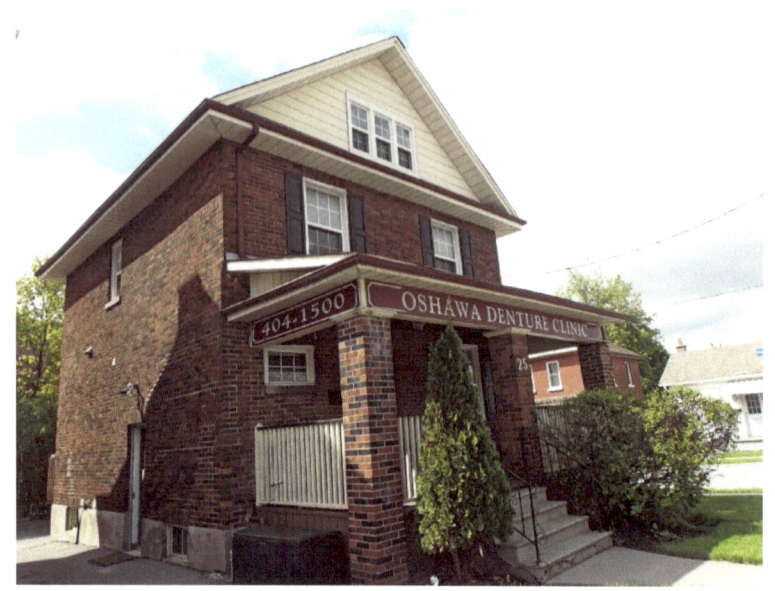

25 Brock Street West - 1914

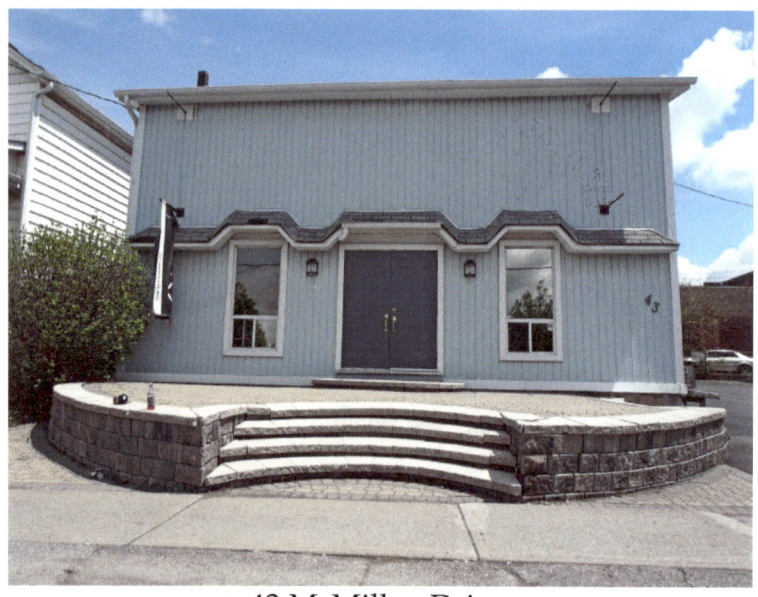

43 McMillan Drive

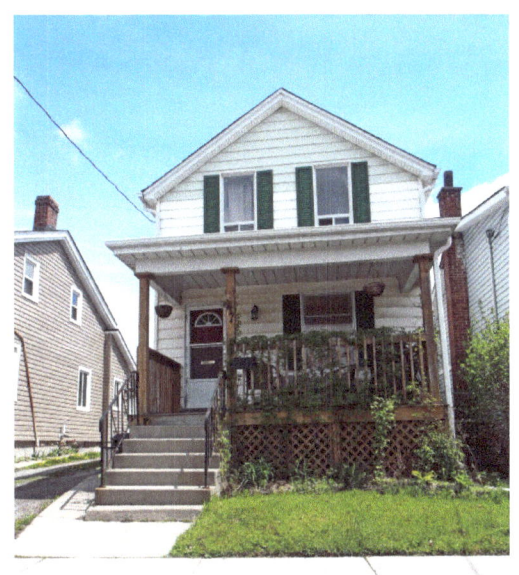

47 McMillan Drive

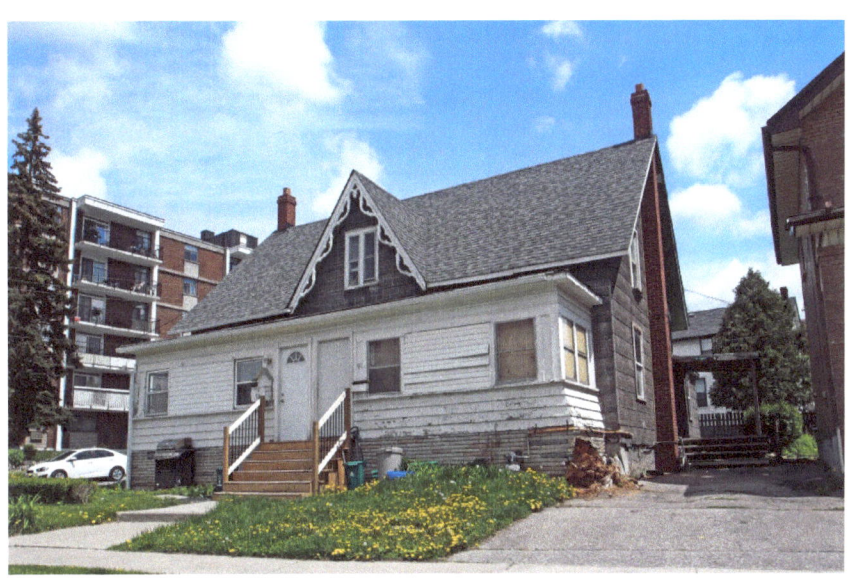

91 McMillan Drive – 1895 - – bargeboard trim on gables

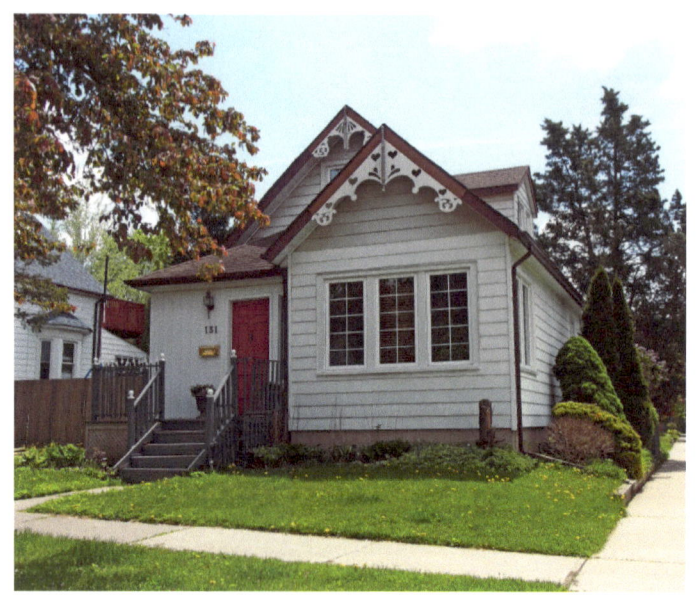

131 Alma Street – bargeboard trim on gables

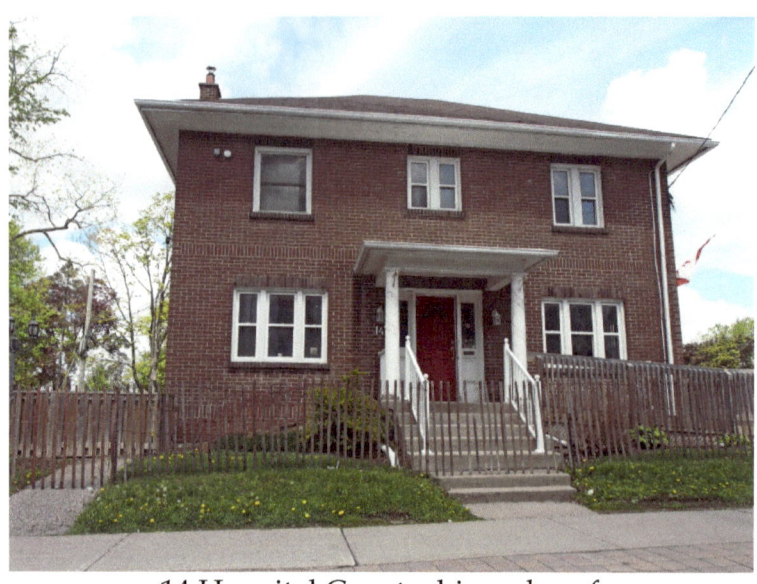

14 Hospital Court – hipped roof

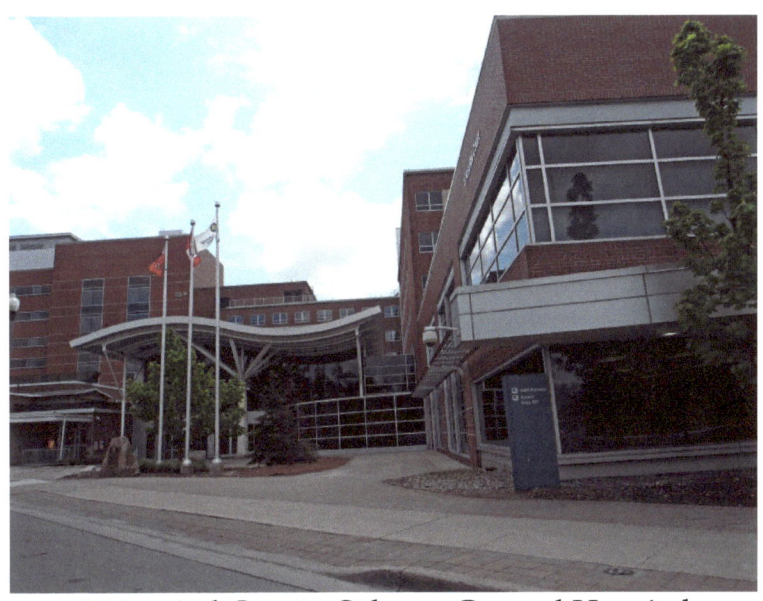

1 Hospital Court - Oshawa General Hospital

William A. Holland joined the hospital in 1945 and served for over 35 years until his death in 1982. During his tenure, Bill was chiefly responsible for three major expansions as the hospital grew from 194 beds to over 650 beds together with a wide-range of out-patient and medical services. Mr. Holland advocated that the hospital's goal was to provide high quality care to all patients and that every employee had an important role to play in achieving this objective.

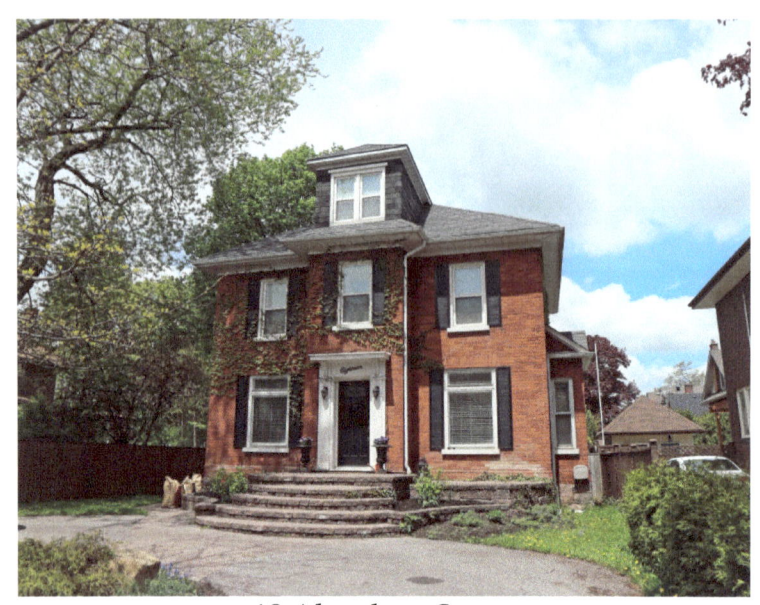
18 Aberdeen Street

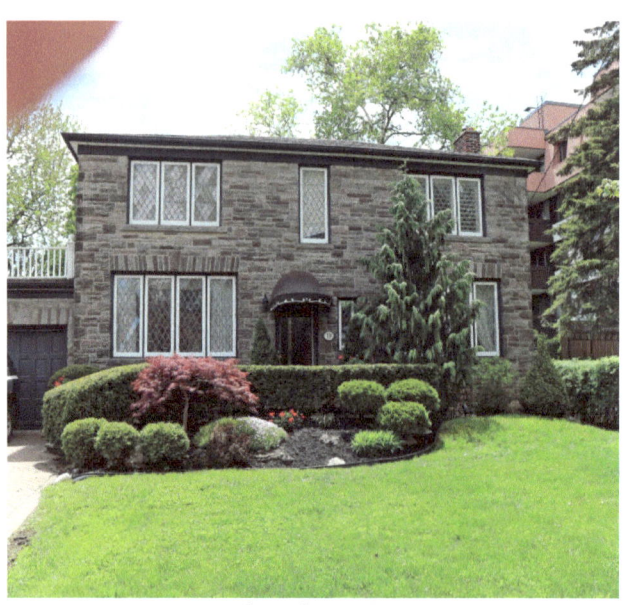
19 Aberdeen Street

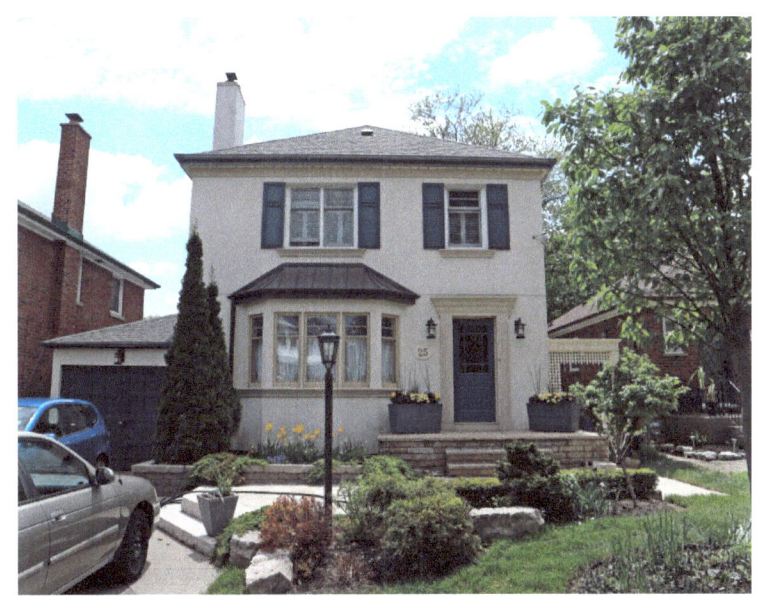

25 Aberdeen Street

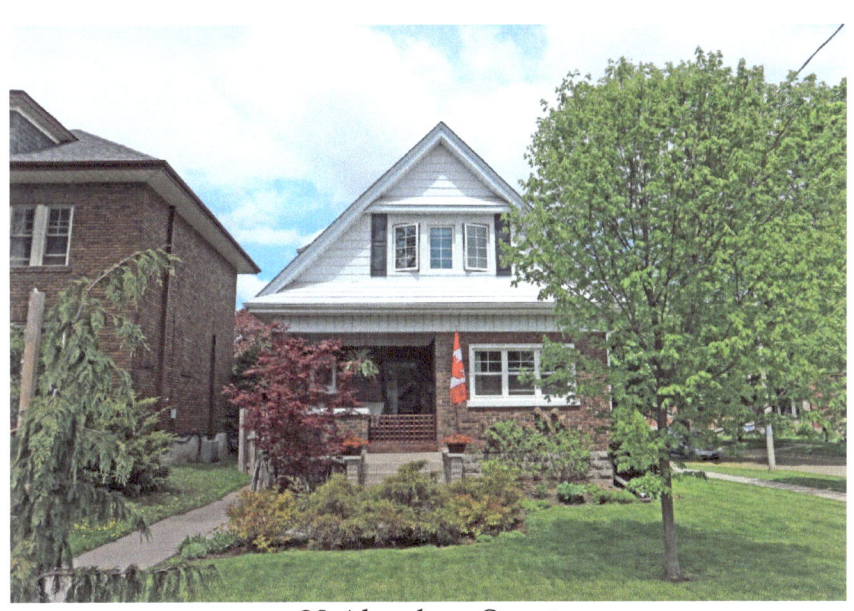

28 Aberdeen Street

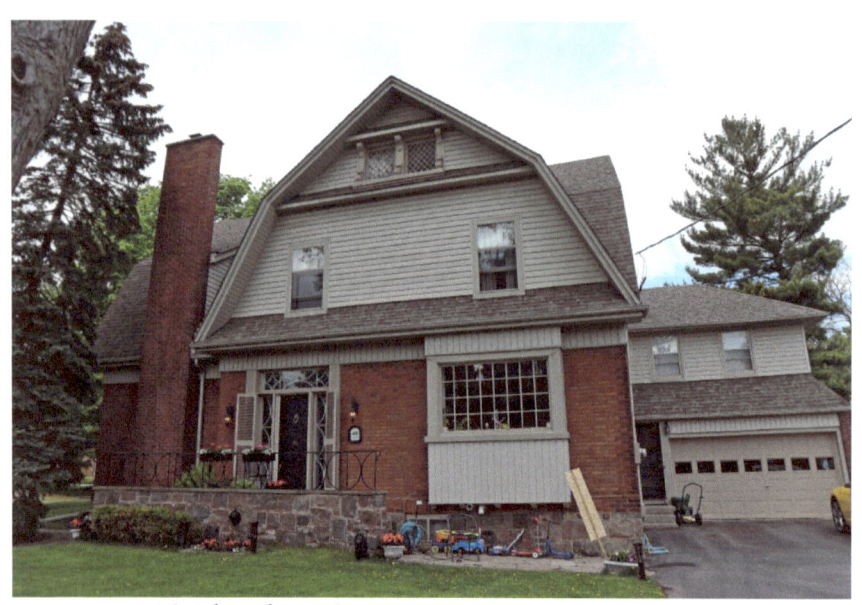

46 Aberdeen Street – 1915 – gambrel roof

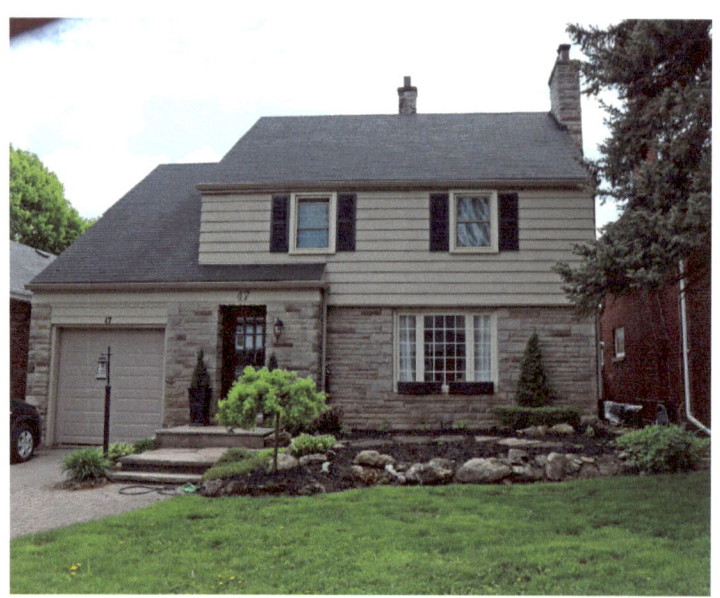

47 Aberdeen Street - 1943

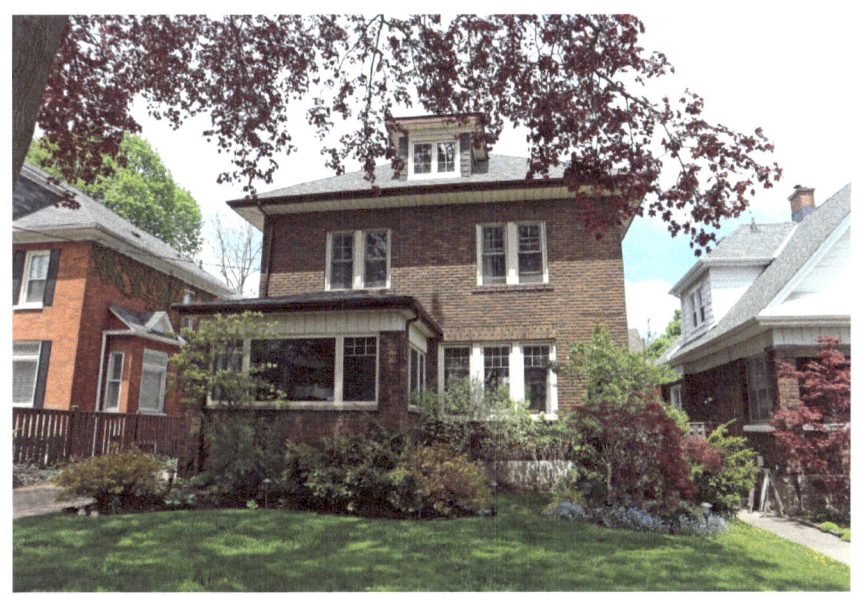

Aberdeen Street

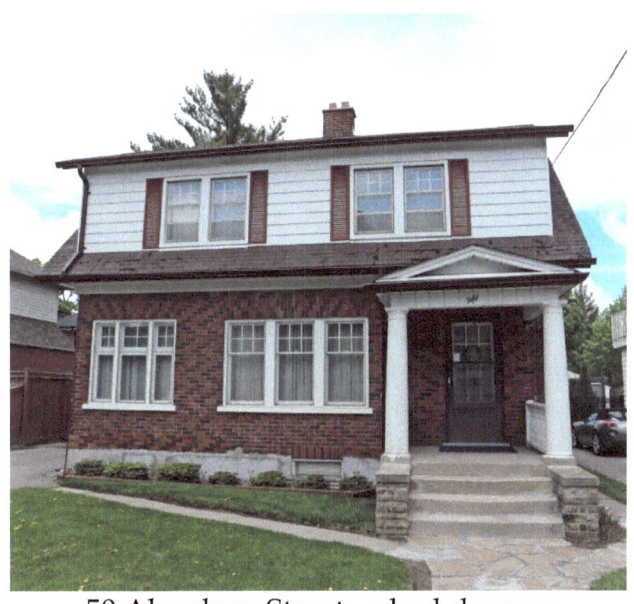

50 Aberdeen Street – shed dormer

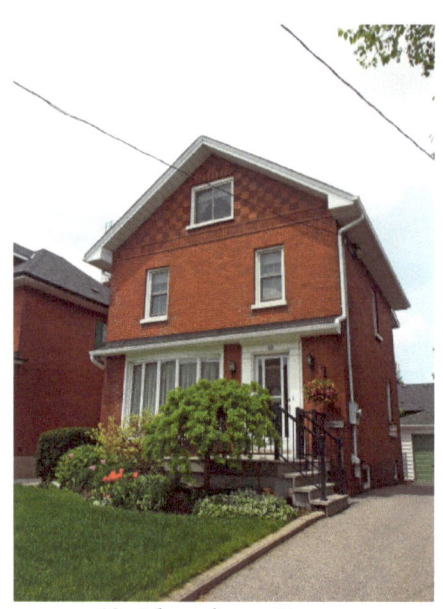

62 Aberdeen Street

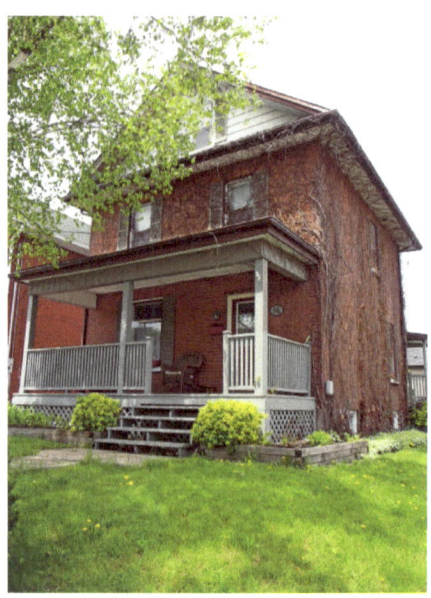

66 Aberdeen Street

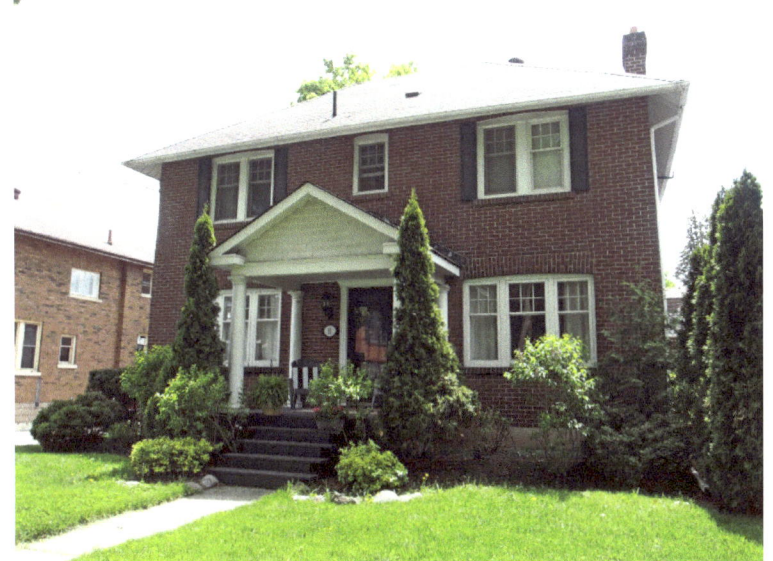

11 Connaught Street

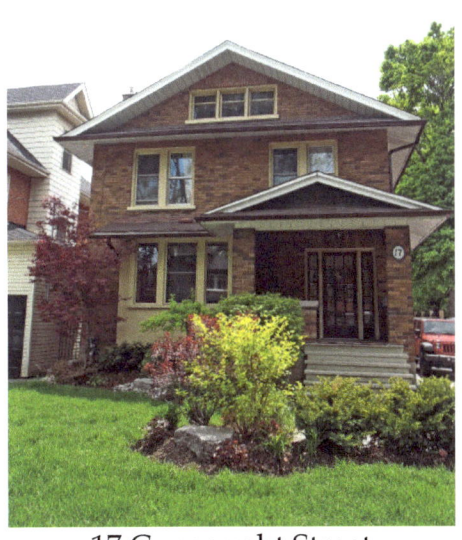

17 Connaught Street

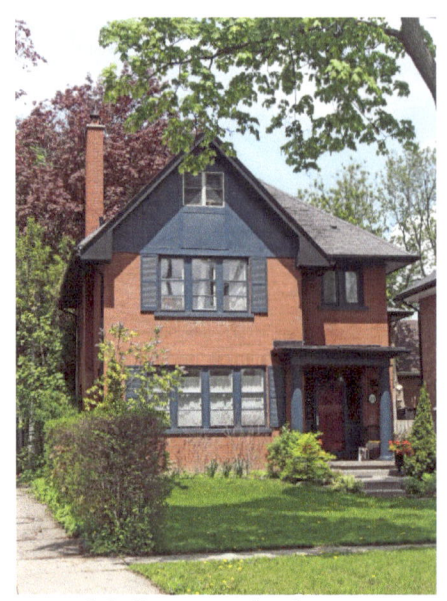

20 Connaught Street

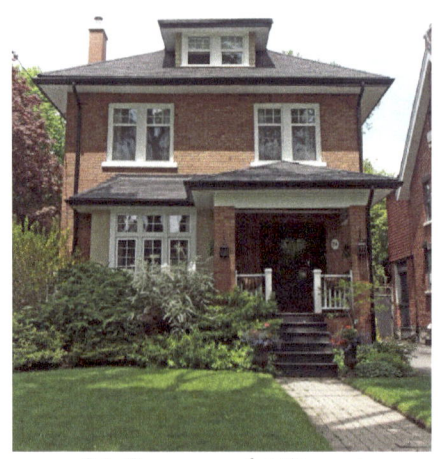

24 Connaught Street

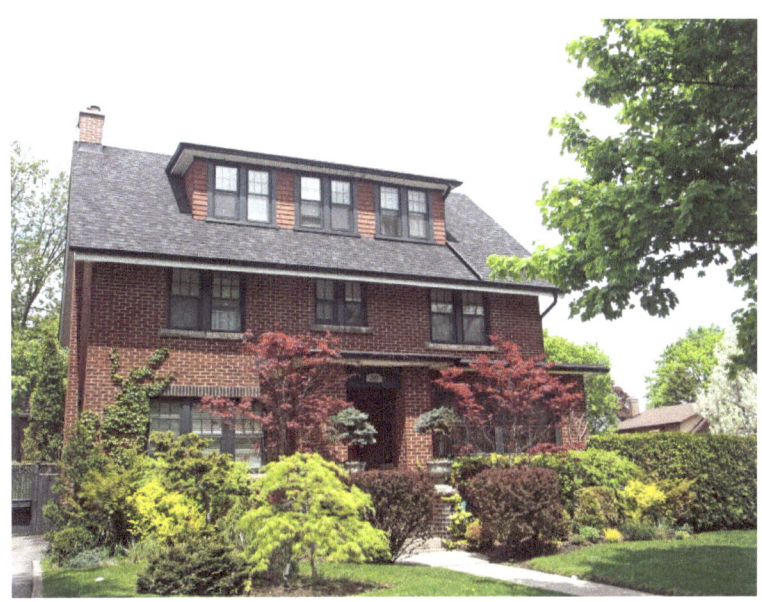
30 Connaught Street – shed dormer in attic

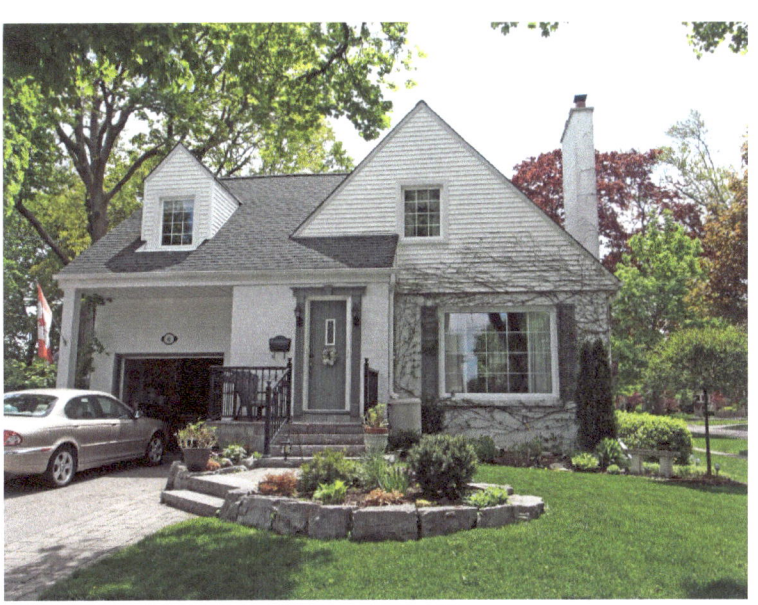
41 Connaught Street

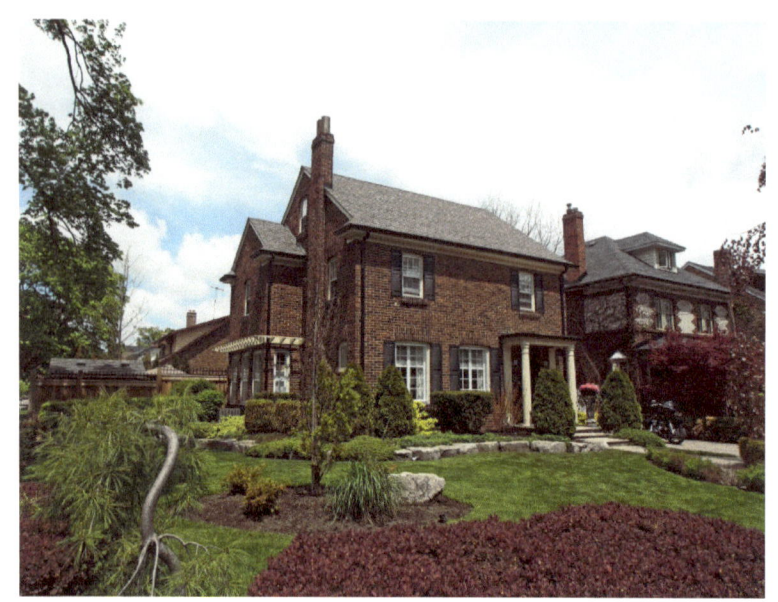

42 Connaught Street

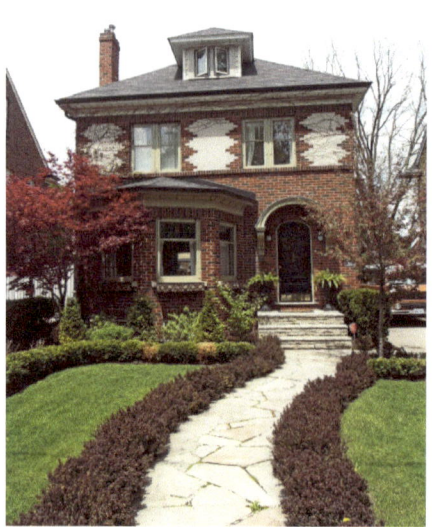

43 Connaught Street

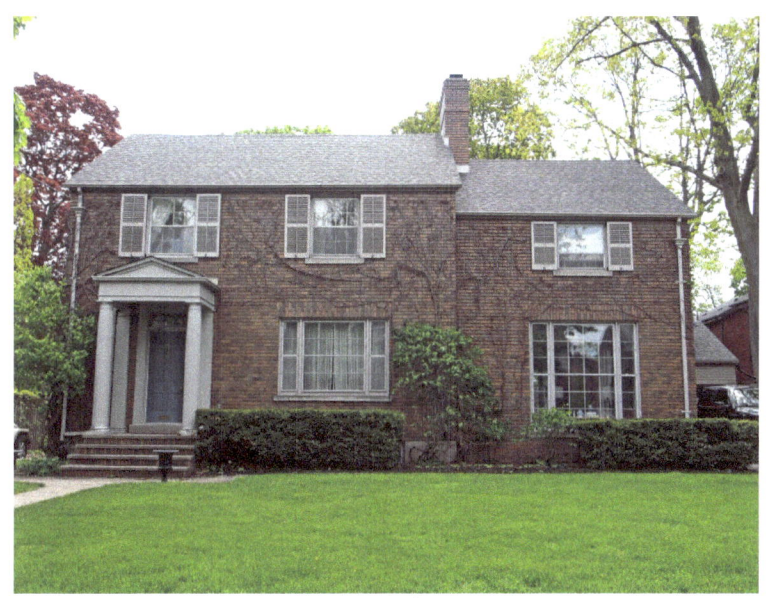

45 Connaught Street

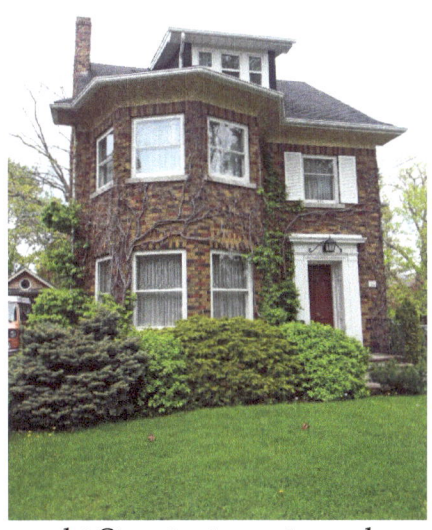

50 Connaught Street – two-storey bay window

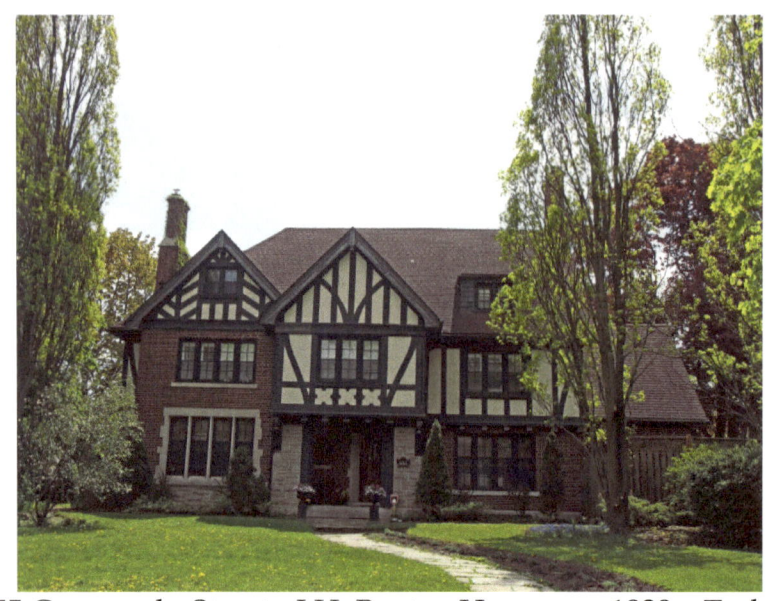

55 Connaught Street - J.H. Beaton House – c. 1928 – Tudor style

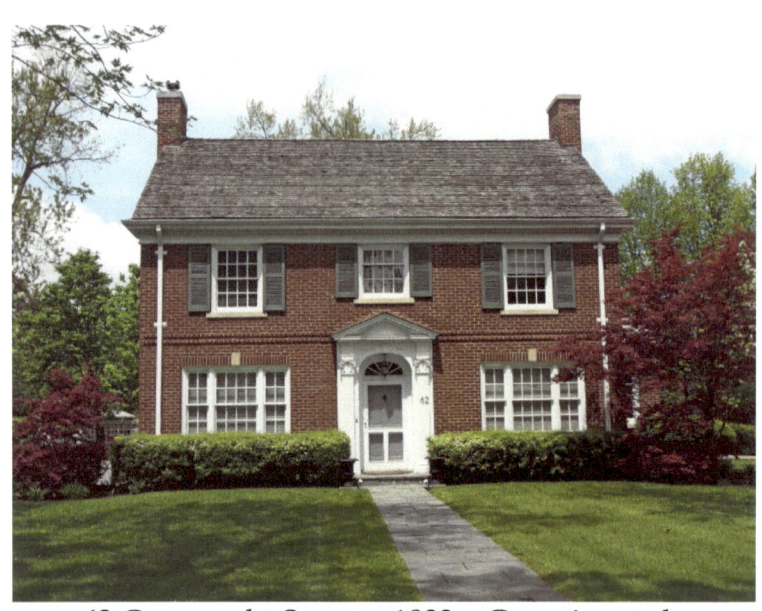

62 Connaught Street – 1923 – Georgian style

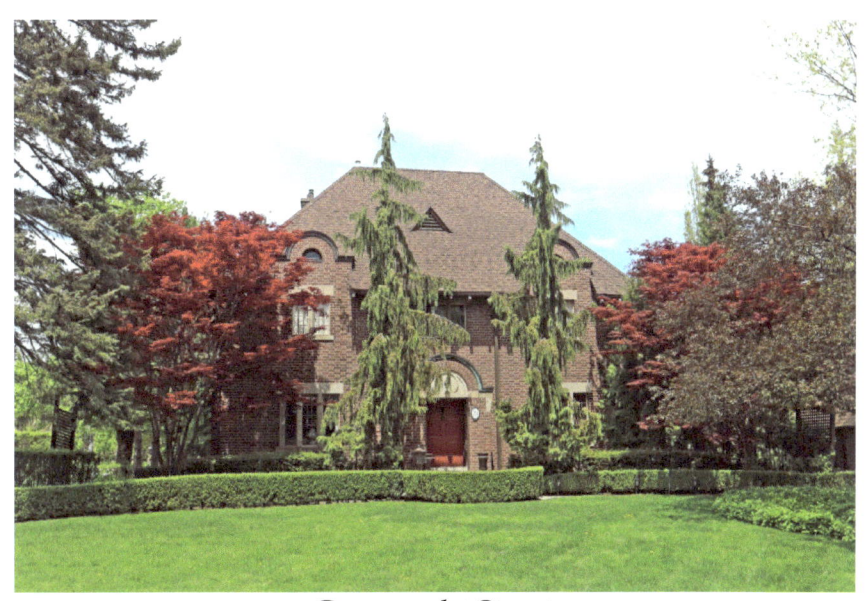

Connaught Street

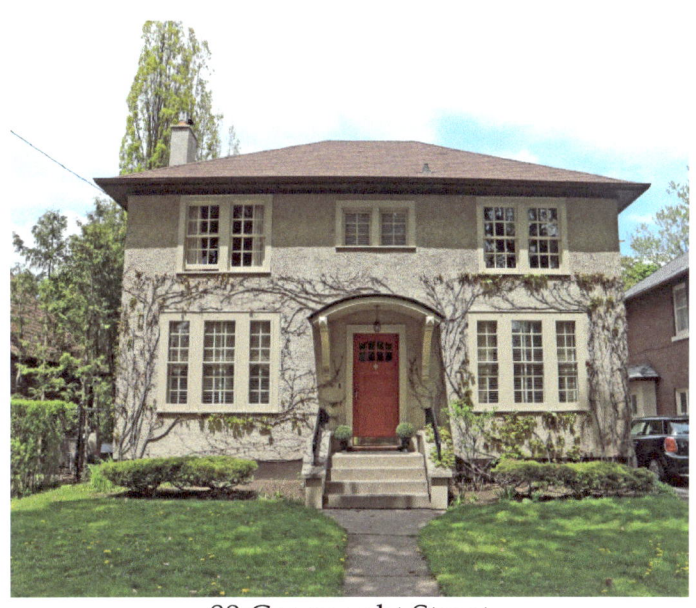

88 Connaught Street

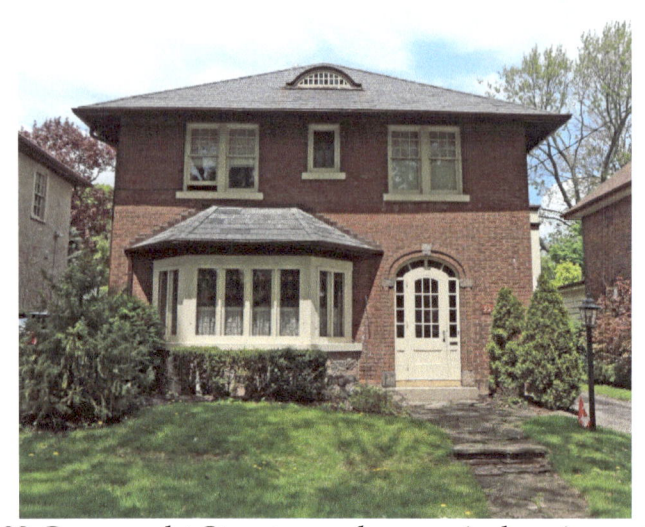

92 Connaught Street – eyebrow window in roof

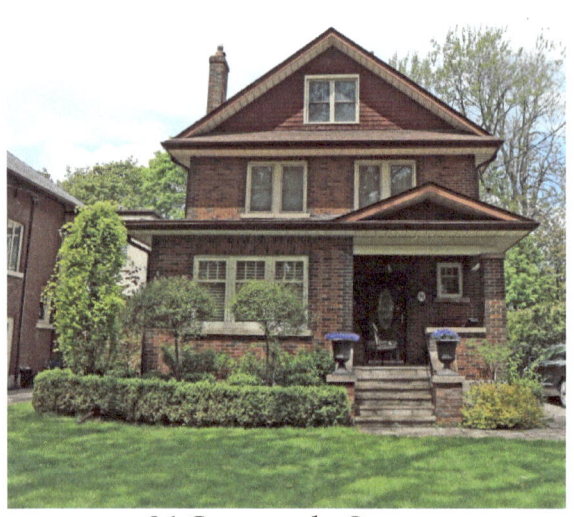

96 Connaught Street

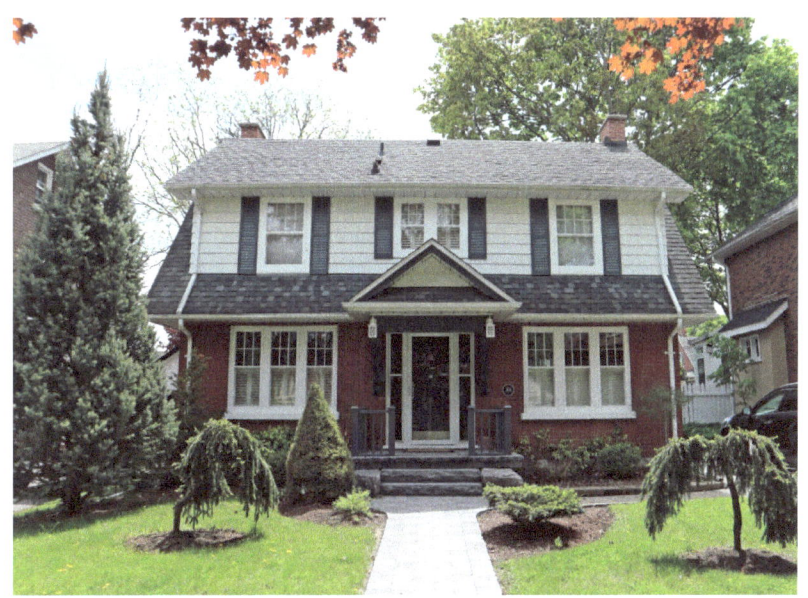

99 Connaught Street – shed dormer

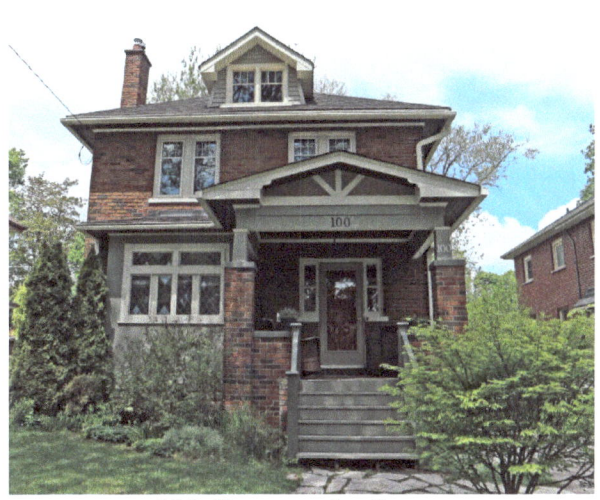

100 Connaught Street

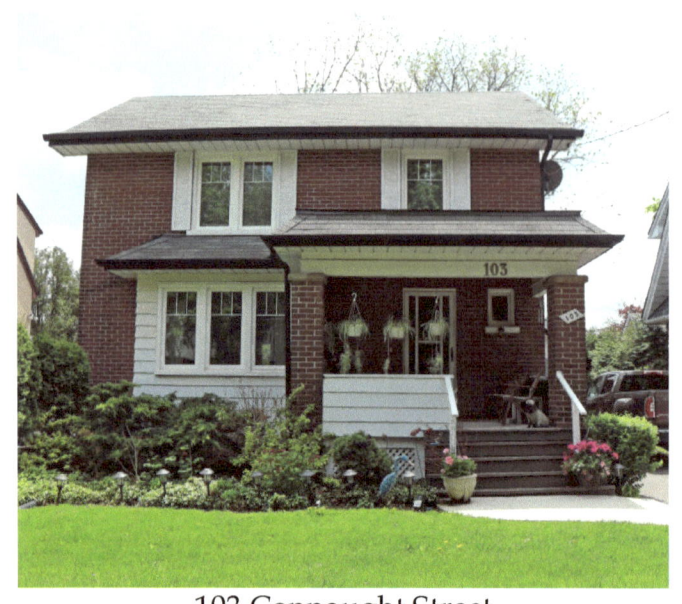

103 Connaught Street

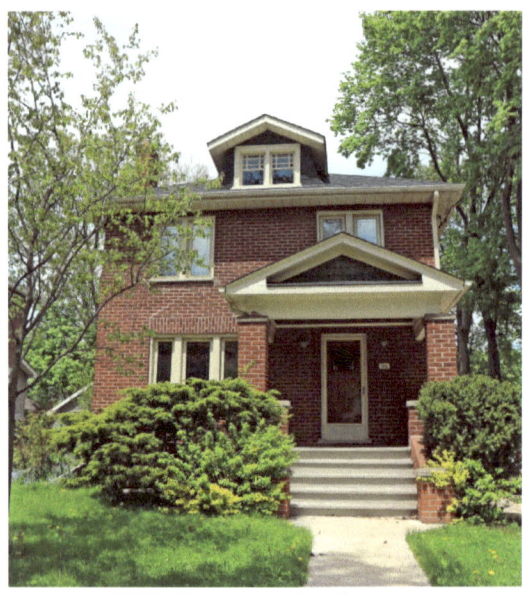

106 Connaught Street

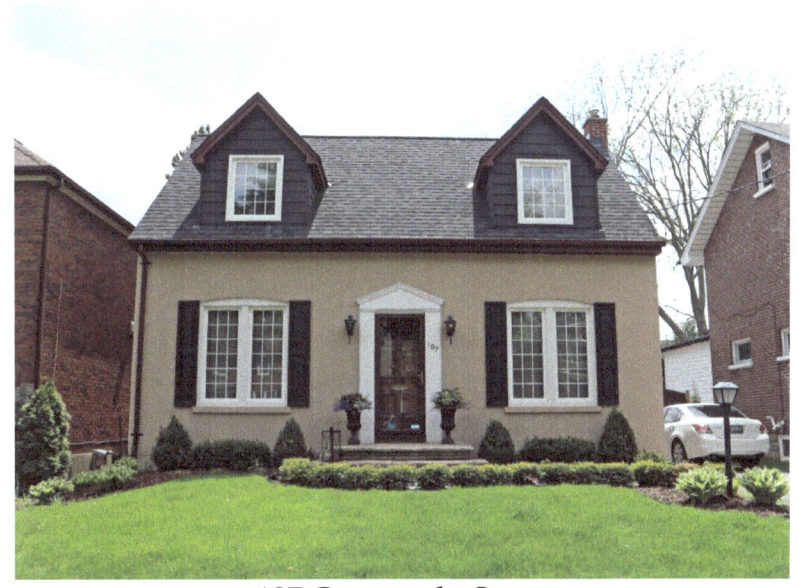

107 Connaught Street

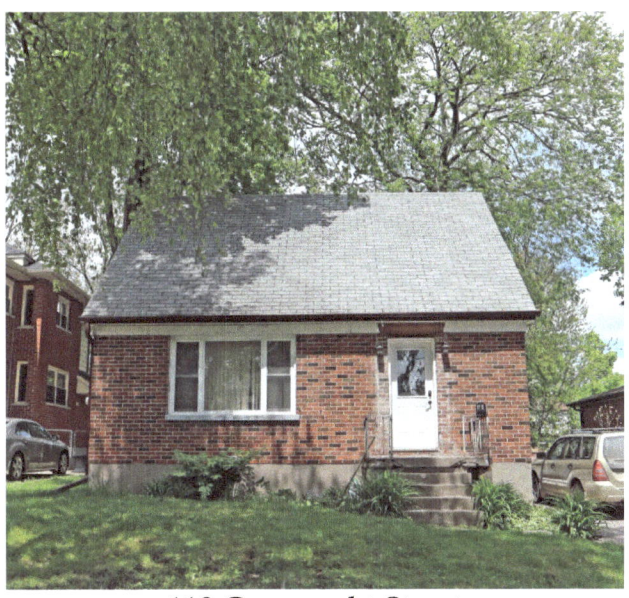

110 Connaught Street

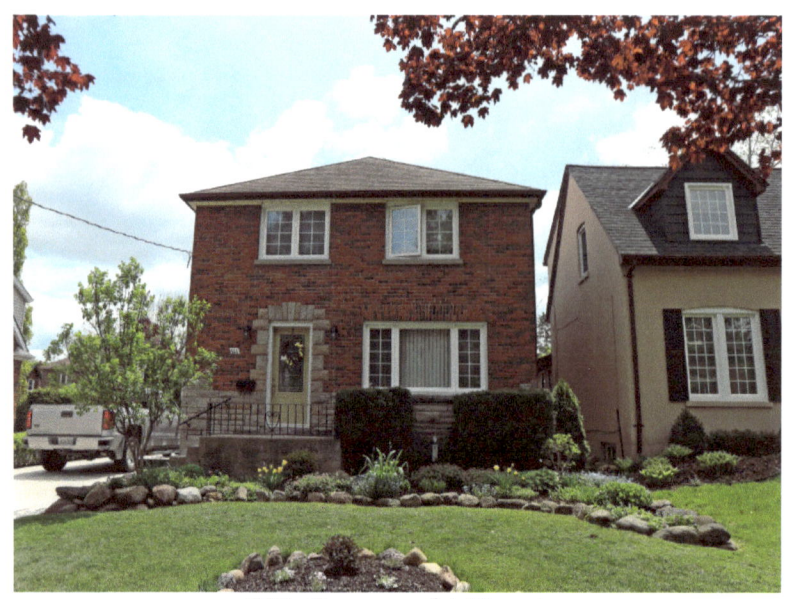

111 Connaught Street

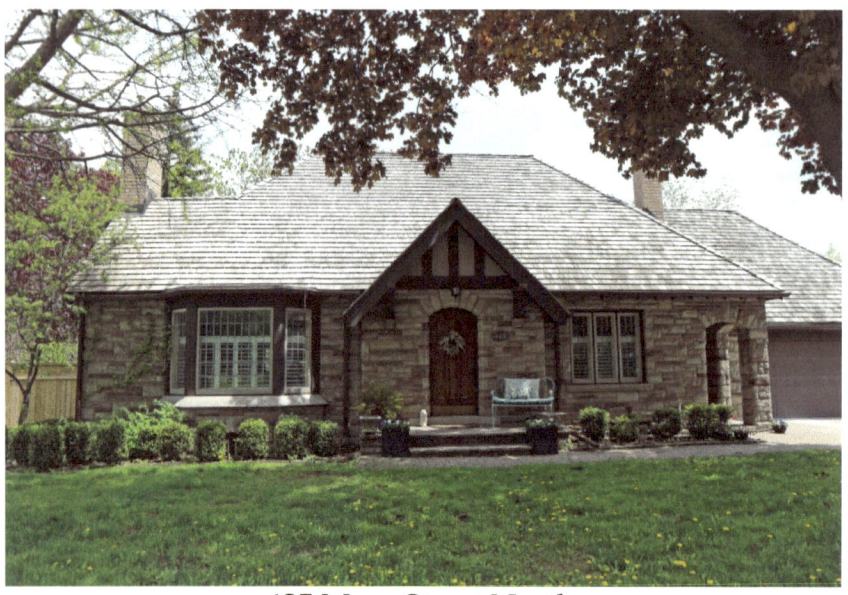

425 Mary Street North

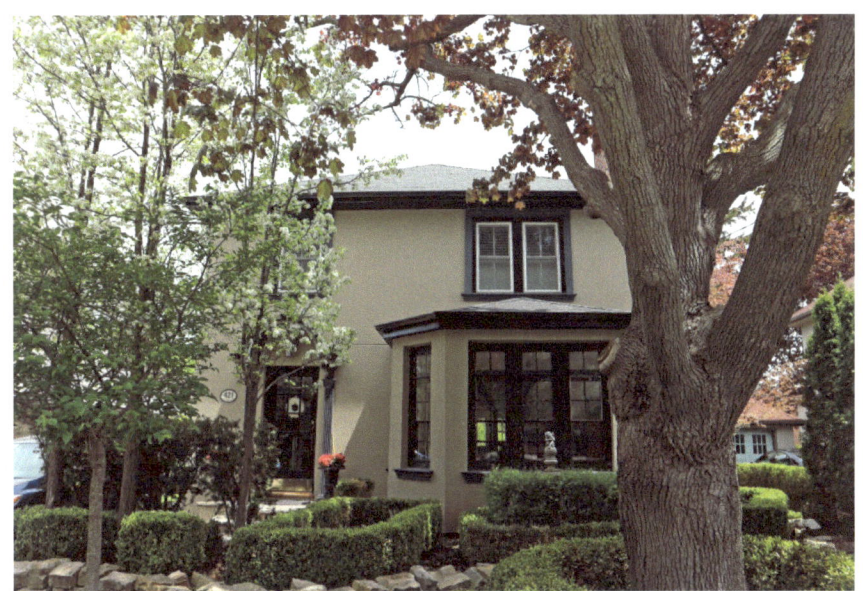

421 Mary Street North

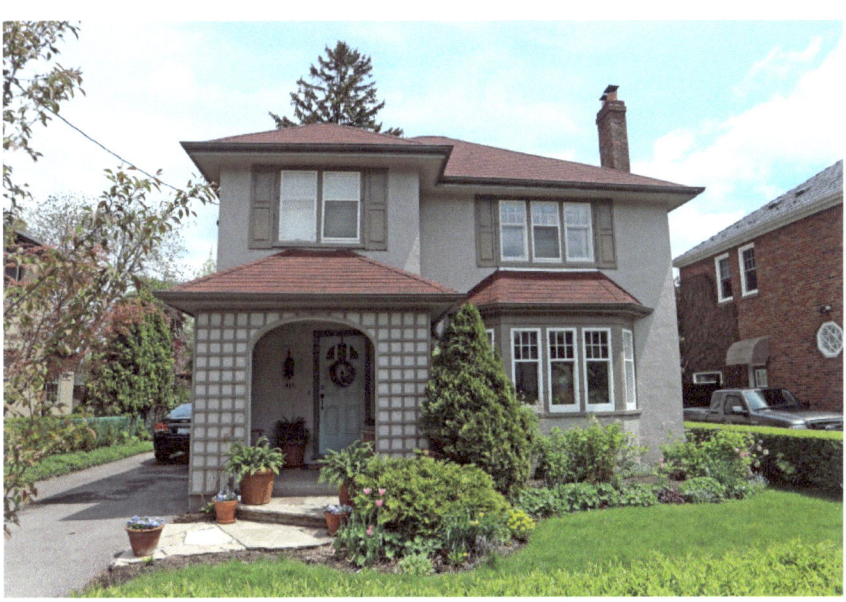

417 Mary Street North

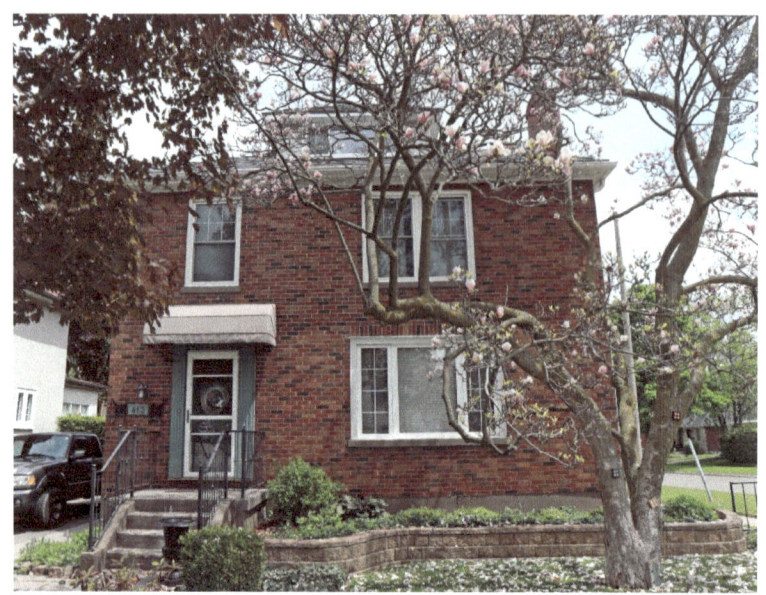

413 Mary Street North

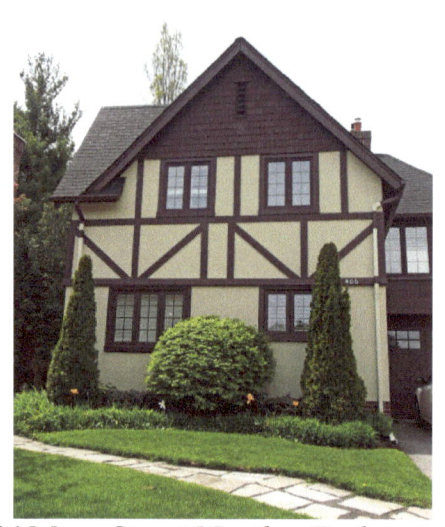

406 Mary Street North – Tudor style

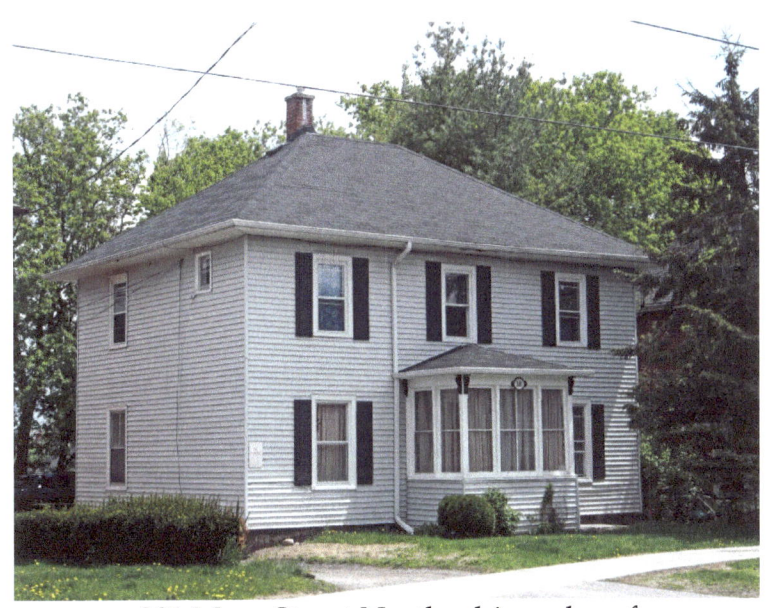

381 Mary Street North – hipped roof

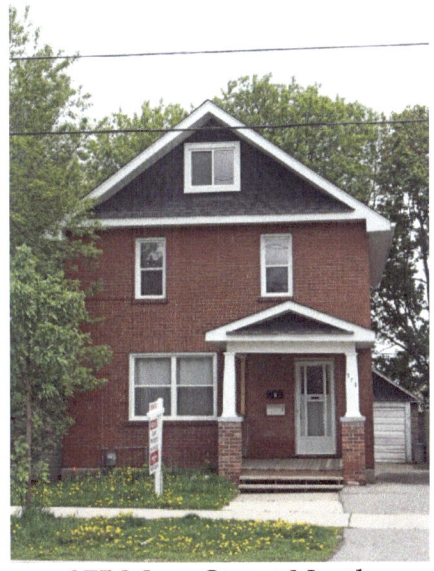

375 Mary Street North

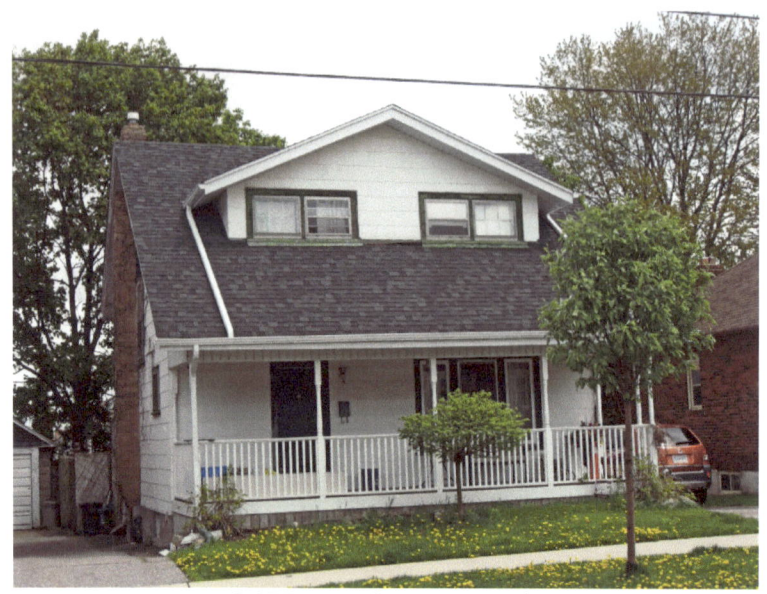

369 Mary Street North

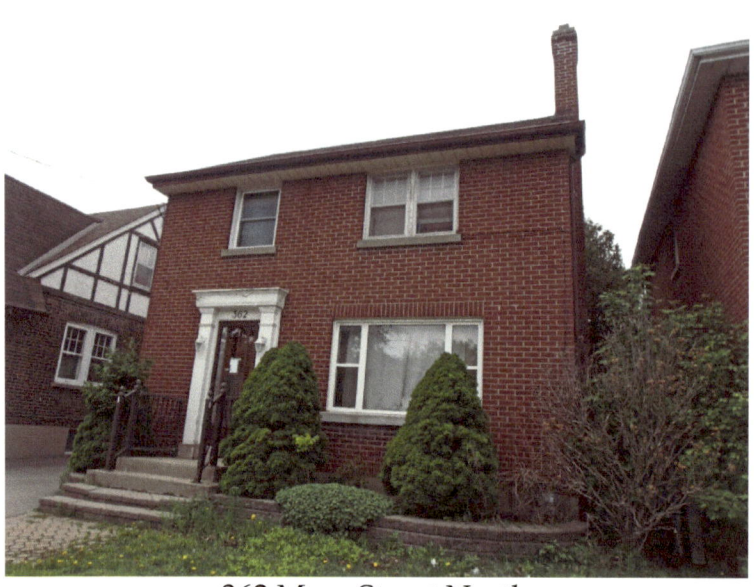

362 Mary Street North

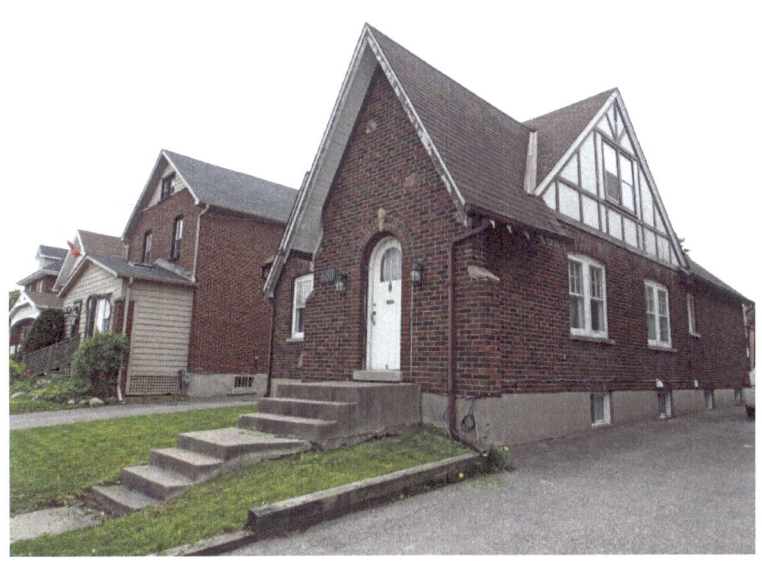

360 Mary Street North - 1939

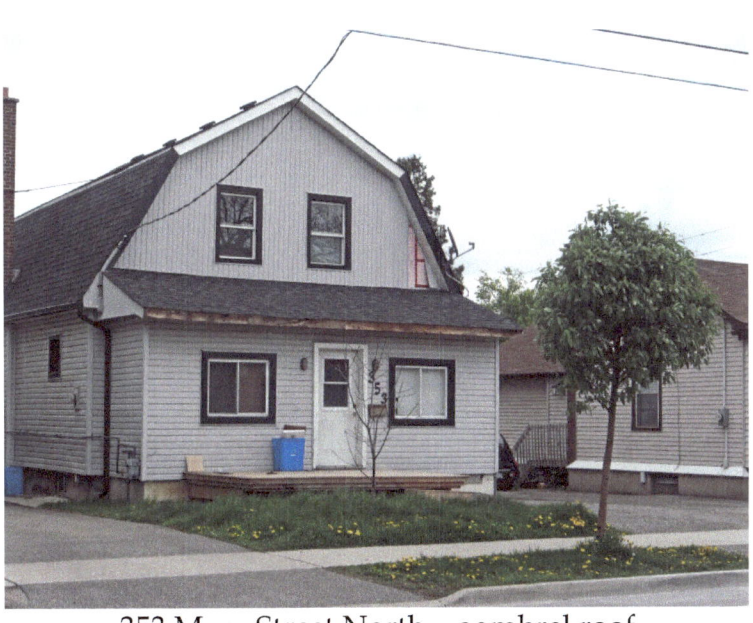

353 Mary Street North – gambrel roof

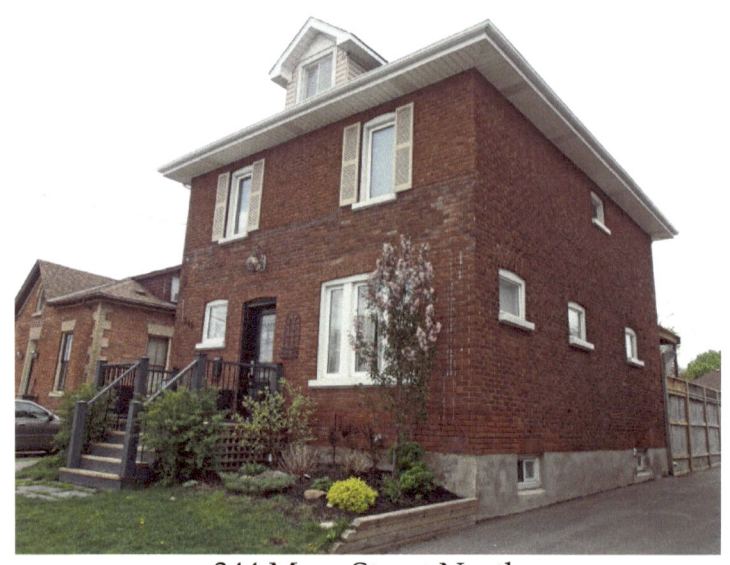

344 Mary Street North

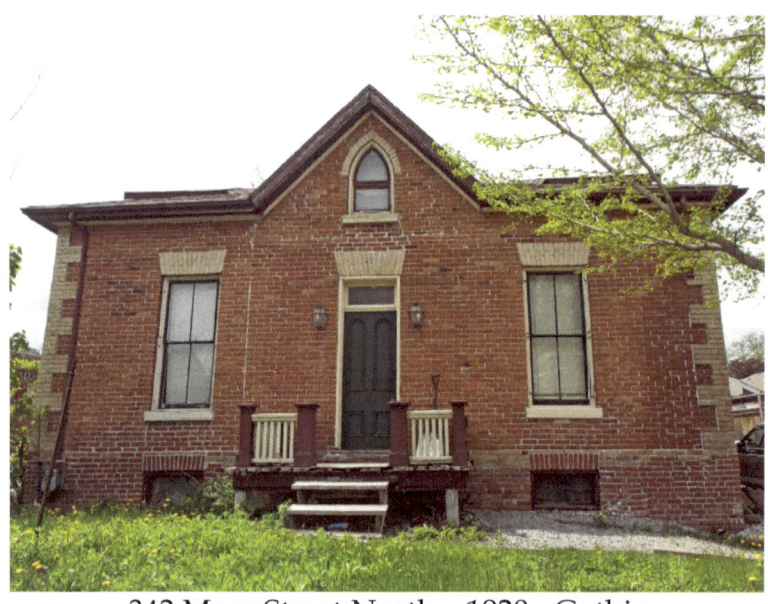

342 Mary Street North – 1920 - Gothic

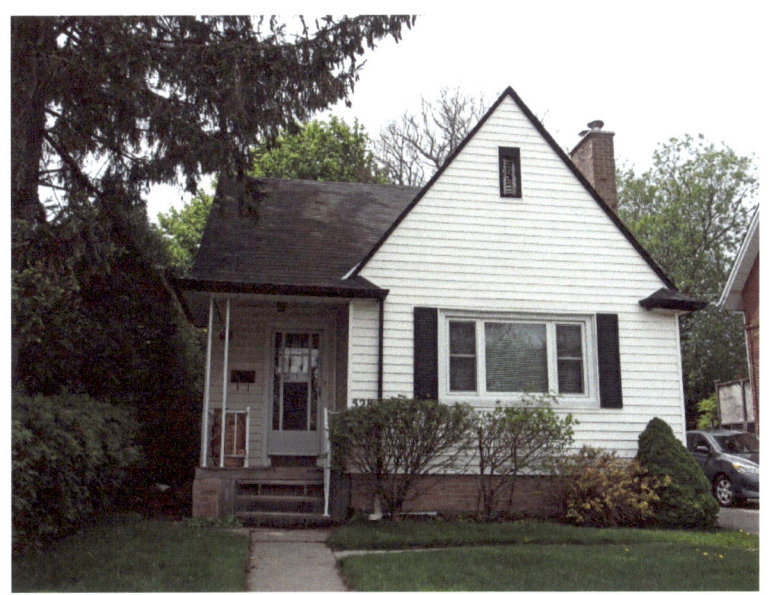

528 Grierson Street

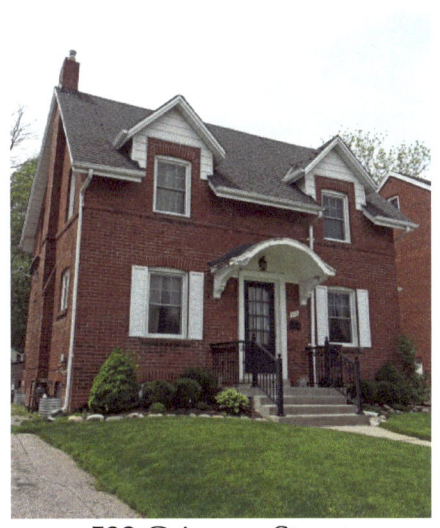

532 Grierson Street

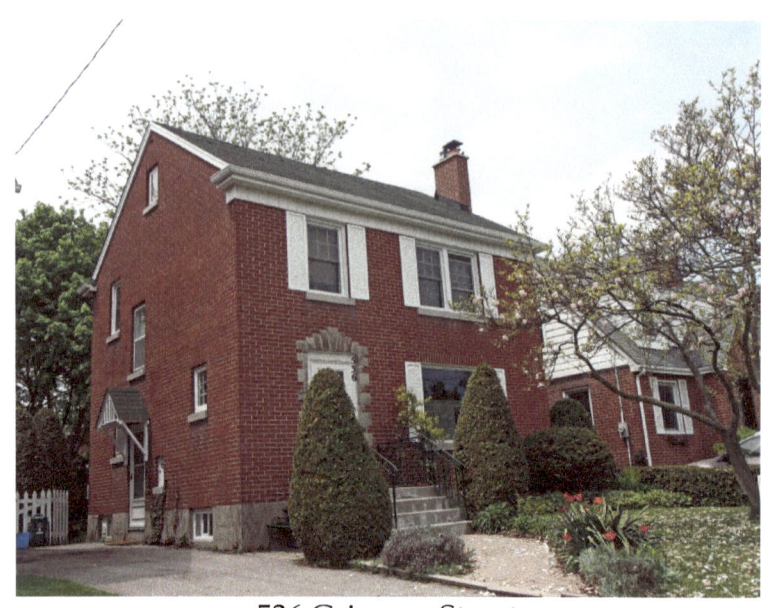

536 Grierson Street

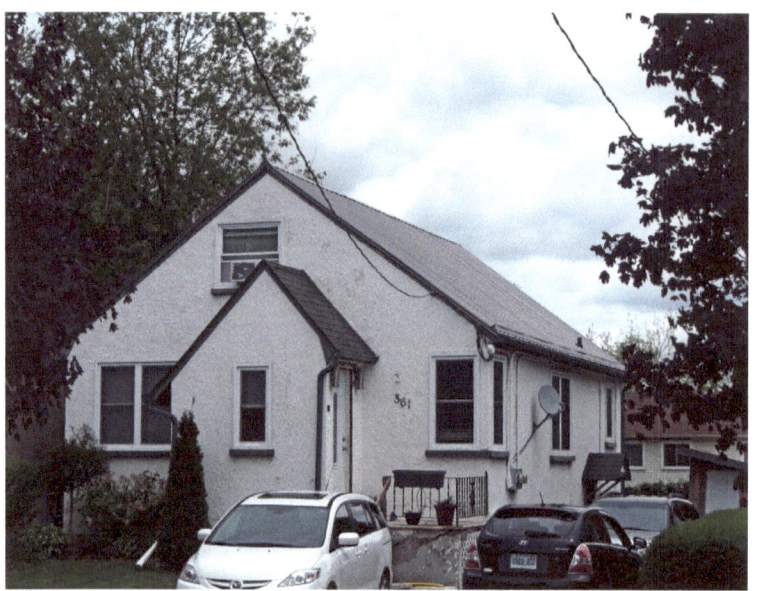

561 Grierson Street

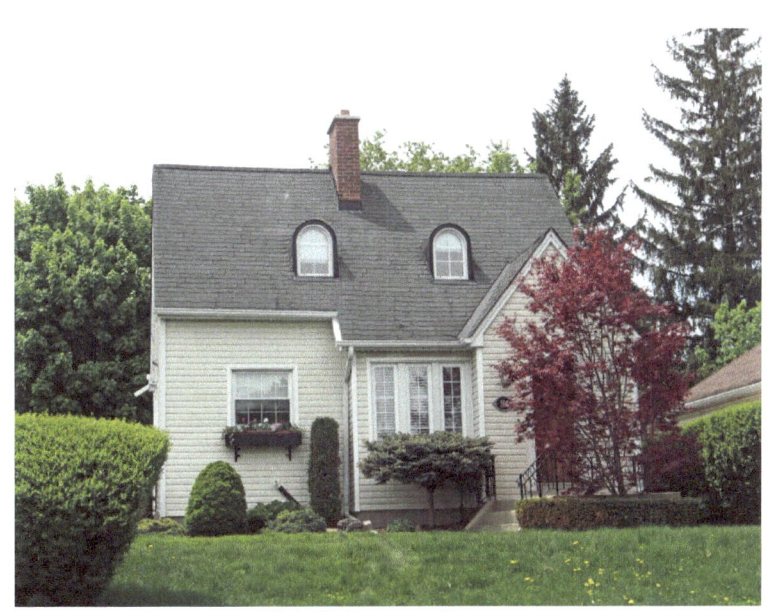

594 Grierson Street

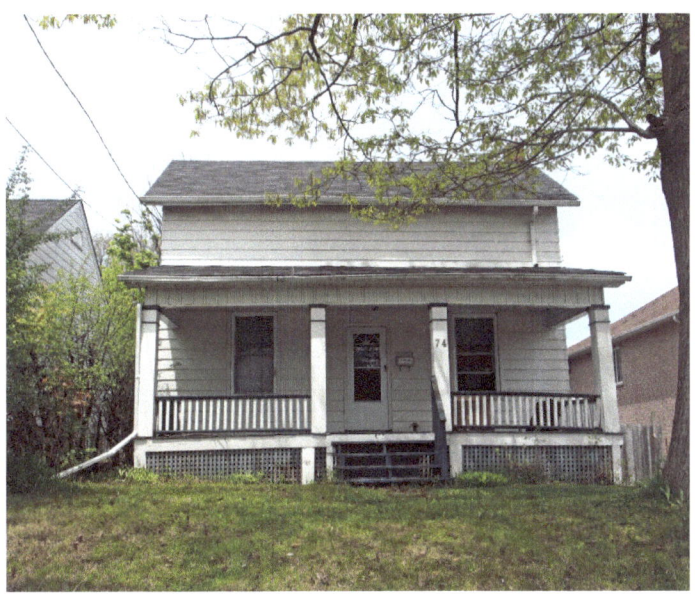

74 Rossland Road East - 1855

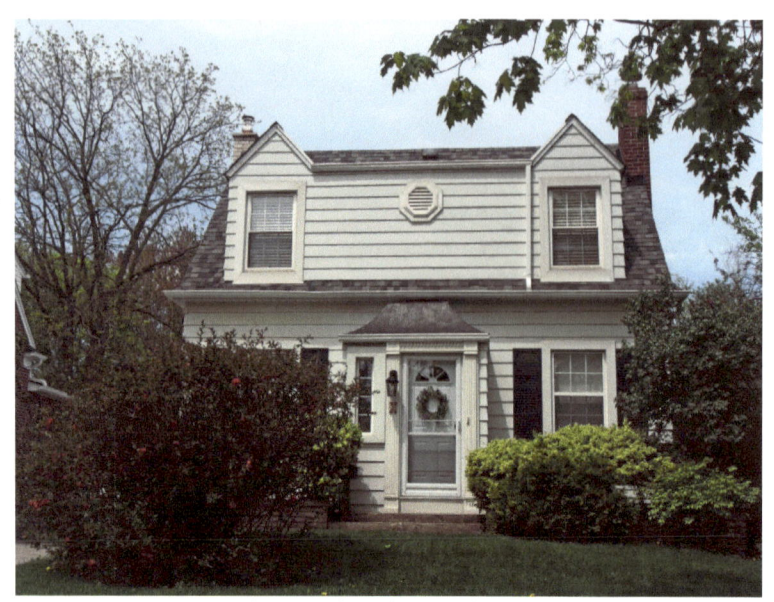

58 Rossland Road East

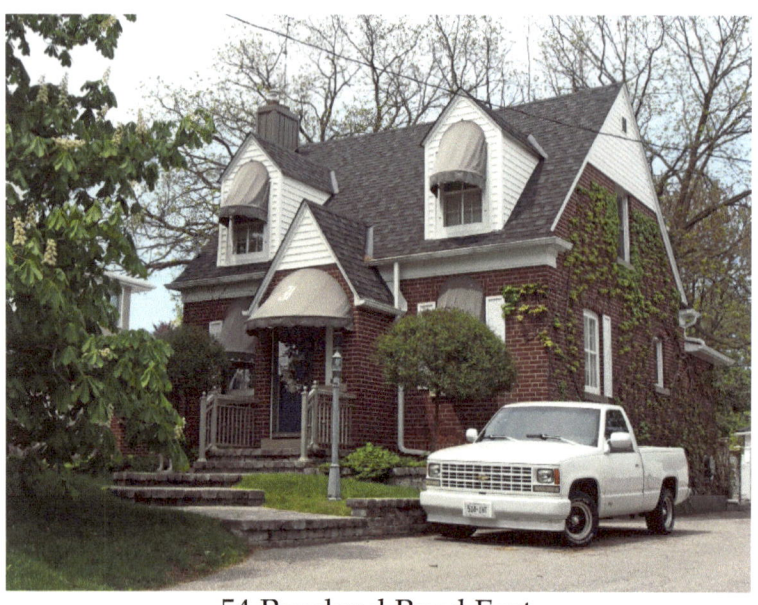

54 Rossland Road East

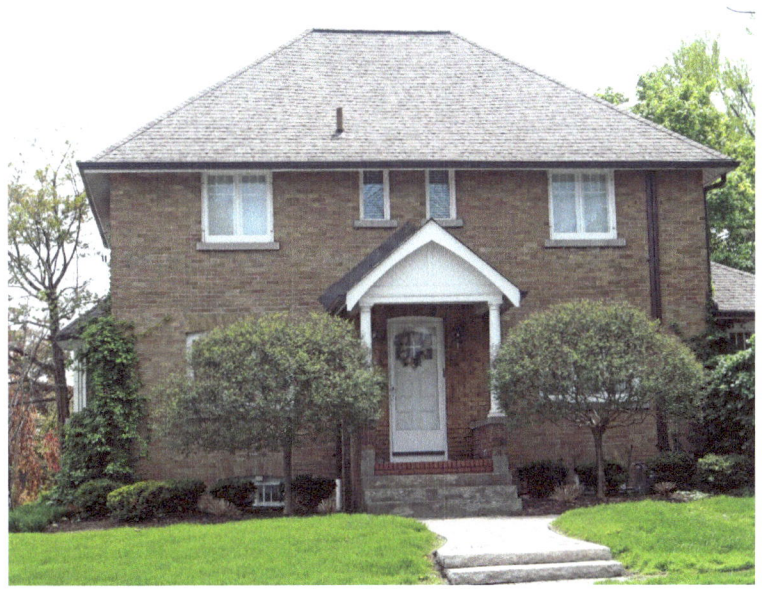

Rossland Road East

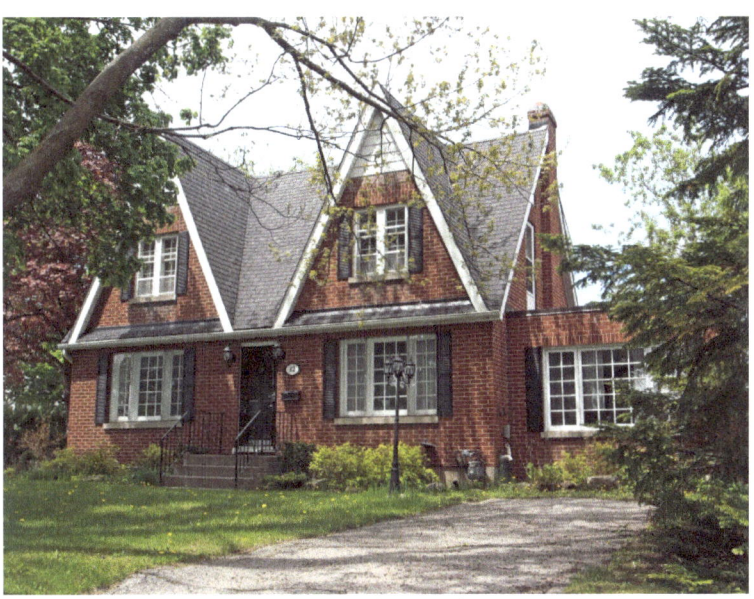

42 Rossland Road East

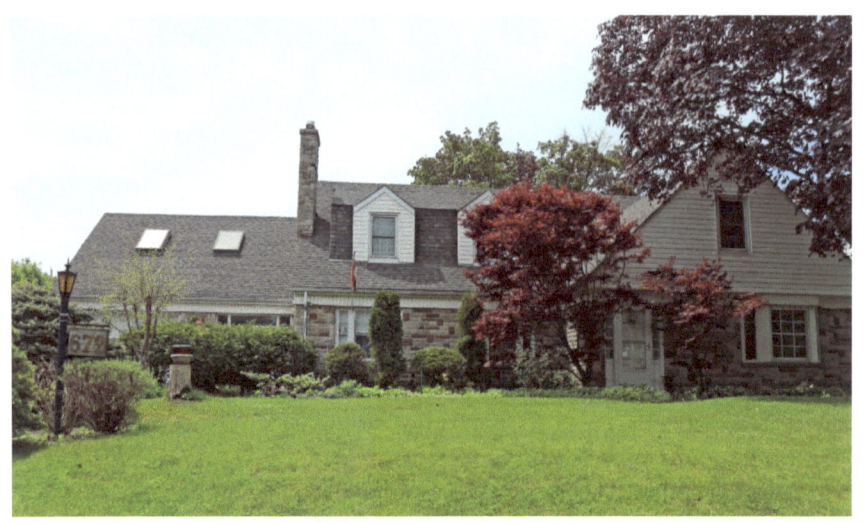

689 Masson Street

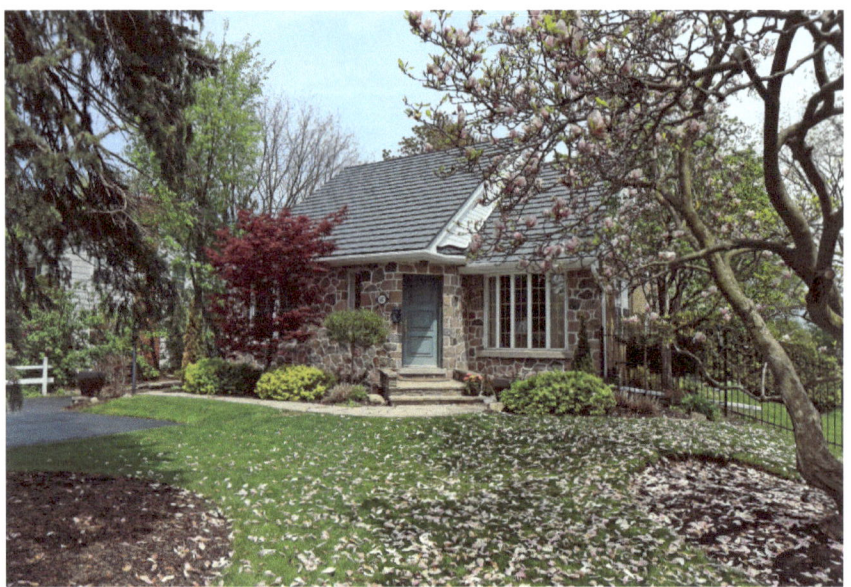

687 Masson Street

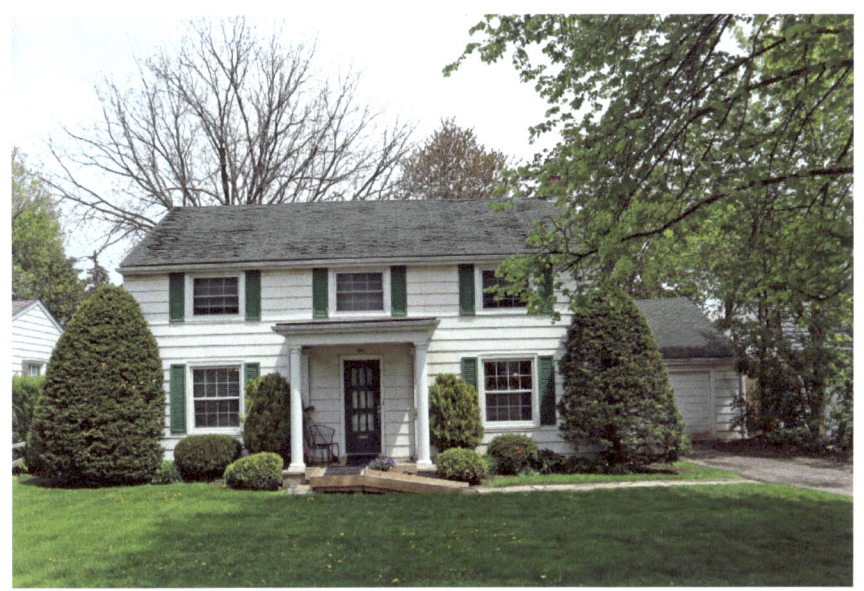

695 Masson Street

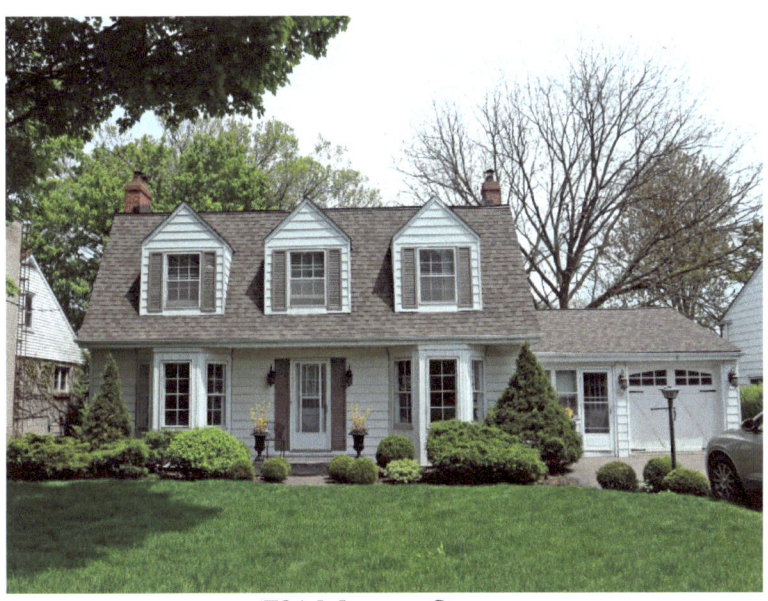

701 Masson Street

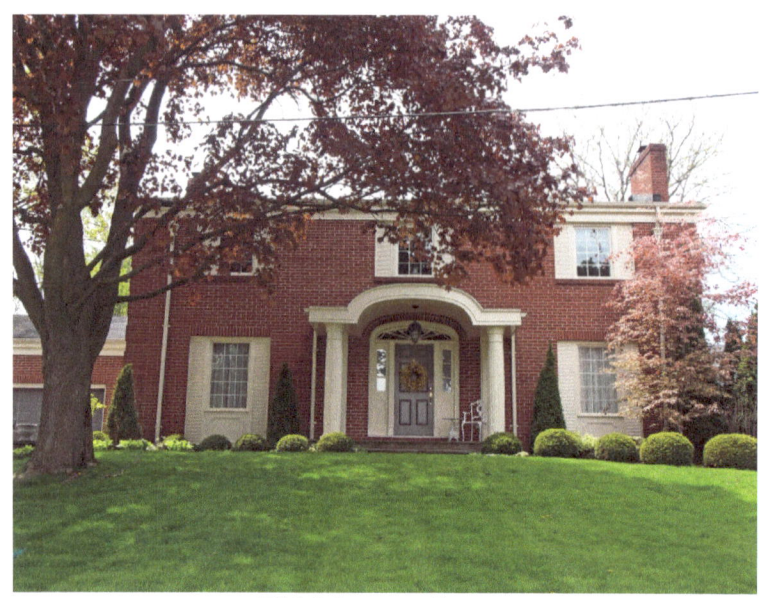

738 Masson Street

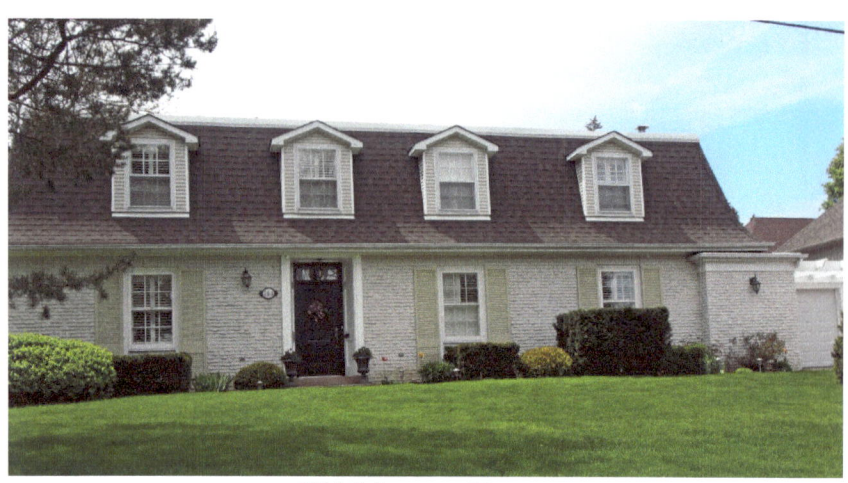

744 Masson Street

Building Styles

Georgian, before 1860 – This style began with the British King Georges in the 18th century. These buildings have balanced facades around a central door, medium-pitched gable roofs, and small paned windows.

Gothic Revival, 1830-1890 – These decorative buildings have sharply-pitched gables with highly detailed verge boards, pointed-arch window openings, and dichromatic brickwork. It is a common style in Ontario.

Neo-Colonial (also Colonial Revival, Georgian Revival or Neo-Georgian) architecture seeks to revive elements of architectural style of American colonial architecture of the period around the Revolutionary War which drew strongly from Georgian architecture of Great Britain. Architecture from the 18th and early 19th centuries in Ontario includes a wide assortment of detailing and ornament applied to a design centered around the fireplace and the source of water. Structures are typically two stories, have a symmetrical front facade with elaborate front doorways, often with decorative crown pediments, fanlights, and sidelights, symmetrical windows flanking the front entrance, often in pairs or threes, and columned porches.

Neo-Gothic (Collegiate Gothic): is monochromatic and on a much grander scale than Gothic. Early Neo-Gothic was the decorative use of Gothic elements with a lack of knowledge and understanding of Gothic construction. Neo-Gothic tried to understand the basic principles of Gothic and used them. Early neo-Gothic churches were often plastered or painted, later neo-Gothic churches were not. An important moment in the development of neo-Gothic is the year 1853, when the hierarchy of the Roman Catholic church was fully restored in the Netherlands. Materials used were natural stone combined with brick. Around the year 1850 neo-Gothicism was maturing and increasingly became a Roman Catholic style almost exclusively. Neo-Gothic was adopted as the style for schools and universities in the early years of the 20th century. The style became so common for scholastic buildings that it is often called Collegiate Gothic. Wall buttresses and finials are added, but they are generally far too small to be of any structural benefit.

Tudor Revival – exposed timbers with stucco infill, multi-paned windows.

Other Books by Barbara Raue

Coins of Gold
Arrows, Indians and Love
The Life and Times of Barbara
The Cromwell Family Book
Laura Secord Discovered
Daddy Where Are You?

Montana Series
Book 1: Montana Dream
Book 2: Life on the Montana Frontier
Book 3: Montana to Boston and Back
Book 4: Montana Sons Go to War
Book 5: Montana Sons Return from War

Donaldson Series
Book 1: Rite of Passage
Book 2: Rite of Marriage

© 2021 by Barbara Raue - All the photos in this book have been taken with my cameras. I own the rights to them.

Barbara is The Authority on Saving Our History One Photo at a Time. She is pursuing her interest in photography and architecture by preserving a record through photos of old buildings from the 1800s and 1900s with their unique architecture. Enjoy the beautiful architecture in the comfort of your living room. Dream about what it was like in those by-gone days. Dream about what it was like to live in a mansion like one of those in this book.

Barbara Raue, a wife, mother and grandmother, is an avid reader and writer. She has researched and compiled several family histories. In 2010, Barbara published her book "Coins of Gold," which celebrates the courageous life of her mother, May Todd. Barbara's second book is a historical fiction "Arrows, Indians and Love" which takes place in Boonesborough, Kentucky during the time of Daniel Boone. In 2013, Barbara published *The Cromwell Family Book* in which she traces her ancestry generations back into Great Britain. Her second novel is called *Laura Secord Discovered*, in which the story of Laura's service during the War of 1812 is shared. Barbara's memoir is titled *Daddy Where Are You?* It tells of her life growing up without a father. Five novels in the Montana Series have been published, *Montana Dream, Life on the Montana Frontier, Montana to Boston and Back, Montana Sons Go to War*, and *Montana Sons Return from War*. The Donaldson series of two novels is available: *Rite of Passage* and *Rite of Marriage*.

This is a link to Barbara's website to view all of her books
http://barbararaue.ca

www.ingramcontent.com/pod-product-compliance
Lightning Source LLC
Chambersburg PA
CBHW040242220526
45473CB00001B/333